Demographic Dynamics in America

THE CHARLES C. MOSKOWITZ MEMORIAL
LECTURES

NUMBER XVIII

Wilbur J. Cohen

Dean of the School of Education
and Professor of Education
and of Public Welfare Administration
University of Michigan

Charles F. Westoff

Director of the Office of Population
Research and Maurice During Professor
of Demographic Studies
Princeton University

Demographic Dynamics in America

The Charles C. Moskowitz Memorial Lectures
College of Business and Public Administration
New York University

THE FREE PRESS
A Division of Macmillan Publishing Co., Inc.
NEW YORK

Collier Macmillan Publishers
LONDON

The Free Press
A Division of Macmillan Publishing Co., Inc.
866 Third Avenue, New York, N.Y. 10022

Collier Macmillan Canada, Ltd.

Library of Congress Catalog Card Number: 77–80227

Printed in the United States of America

printing number

1   2   3   4   5   6   7   8   9   10

Library of Congress Cataloging in Publication Data
Cohen, Wilbur Joseph
   Demographic dynamics in America.

   (The Charles C. Moskowitz memorial lectures ; no. 18)
      1.   United States--Population--Addresses, essays,
lectures. 2.   Fertility, Human--United States--Addresses,
essays, lectures. 3.   Age--Addresses, essays, lectures.
I.   Westoff, Charles F., joint author. II.   Title.
III.   Series.
HB3505.C64   301.32'9'73   77-80227
ISBN 0-02-905780-9

FOREWORD

The Charles C. Moskowitz Memorial Lectures were established at the College of Business and Public Administration with the purpose of advancing public understanding of issues of major concern to business and to the nation. The donor was the late Charles C. Moskowitz, a remarkably warm, generous, and compassionate human being who was also a distinguished alumnus of the College. He was a pioneer in the American motion picture industry and was one of those who helped develop the film industry from small beginnings to its present position. Through the lecture series the College has been able to magnify its educational scope and to make a significant contribution to public discussion and understanding of important issues affecting the American economy and its business enterprises.

The present volume is the eighteenth in the Charles C. Moskowitz Memorial Lecture Series. All of the lectures have been on topics of great importance and have stimulated lively interest. Most have managed to be in the vanguard of events. They have elucidated major issues which were as yet not clear. The lectures published in this book are in that group, being concerned with the subject of demographic dynamics in the United States. We should all be aware that major population shifts are under way. These shifts will alter greatly the age composition of the population, as well as its geographical distribution across the nation, to mention only two aspects of what is happening. And these changes will have profound impacts, sociologically, economically, politically, and environmentally. They will surely affect the quality of our lives and of the lives of our children. But we are uncertain as to how.

We are grateful that the Moskowitz Memorial Lectures provided a forum for bringing together Wilbur J. Cohen, Dean of the School of Education at the University of Michigan and former Secretary of Health, Education, and Welfare, and Charles F. Westoff, Director of the Office of Population Research and Maurice During Professor of Demographic Studies at Princeton University, to discuss population trends and the important issues inherent in them. We are appreciative also that Ernest Kurnow, Professor of Business Statistics, and Dennis H. Wrong, Professor of Sociology, both of New York University, were available as discussants.

Although there is an unavoidable overlap in the papers presented by Dean Cohen and Professor Westoff, each one focused on different aspects of population trends. Dean Cohen concentrated on the changing age composition of the population, with the proportion of youths (under 20) declining and that of the aged (65 and over) increasing, seeing important impacts in such areas as retirement ages, social security, private pension arrangements, and medical care costs. He observed, however, that the dependency ratio of the population, while it would vary, would do so at lower rates than in the recent past in the United States. The dependency ratio is the proportion of the "nonproductive" age groups in the population (under 20, and 65 and over) to the productive group (20–64), and Dean Cohen expects it to drop to about 65 percent by 2010 and to rise thereafter to 80 percent by 2030. But the ratio was 90 percent in the 1960's and was 86.1 percent as recently as 1973.

Despite the decline in the dependency ratio, Dean Cohen sees the major social policy issue before us summed up in this question: How can we provide a more satisfactory living level for more aged, while improving health and education for the young, and simultaneously providing additional real income to the working segment of the population? He makes it clear that he believes that a harmonious and constructive answer will require a strengthened role for the family and greater effectiveness in governmental policies and actions at all levels (federal, state, and local). In the last connection, it seems to me that he displays great faith in the ultimate efficacy of social programs by government, in spite of the major failures he observes as having characterized state and local activities in the past.

Professor Westoff concentrated on the decline in fertility, which has recently been so sharp and so much a subject of discussion and, in some quarters, concern. Of course, the drop in fertility underlies the massive changes in the age composition of the population, which is the main concern of Dean Cohen's remarks. But Professor Westoff's eyes perceive further dimensions. He observes that the fertility decline represents a return to a two-century trend in the United States, and that it is paralleled by a similar experience in other industrialized societies. Thus, he sees the "baby boom" of the 'fifties as the aberration in our population record. Viewed this way, one's attention is turned to the underlying and long-term forces affecting fertility. These are: (1) massive postponement of marriage, and possibly a fundamental shift in the institution and its relationship to childbearing; (2) the changing status and role of women, and their changing attitudes toward marriage, work, and childbearing; and (3) the enormous improvements that have taken place in birth control technology and its wide diffusion in the population.

Examining the economic, environmental, political, and social consequences of the present low American fertility rate, Professor Westoff sees a stationary population as quite possible within four decades, and perhaps even a declining population thereafter. After all, population replacement requires an average lifetime number of children per woman of two, while the present rate is 1.8. But this outlook does not disturb him, for he sees in it substantially reduced adverse pressures on our economy, our environment, our political system, and our social system. In particular, he is optimistic with respect to the outlook for the "dependency ratio." And in this he seems generally more optimistic in his outlook than is Dean Cohen. But he seems significantly less optimistic with respect to the outlook for the institutions of marriage and the family. He notes later marriages, greater cohabitation and childbearing outside of wedlock, increased independence of women, and lessened influence of religion. As a consequence, he perceives that "the future seems less and less compatible with long-term traditional marriage." Professor Westoff speculates that the achievement of natural replacement of the American population will require substantial financial incentives to encourage childbearing. But he does not seem too optimistic about that. And he is no more optimistic about American policies being altered so as to encourage larger-scale immigration. In short, our population may be expected to stabilize, or even decline, and we shall have to emphasize improvements in the quantity and quality of life on a per capita rather than on an aggregative basis.

Professors Kurnow and Wrong made incisive critical comments. Professor Kurnow focused on the importance of the assumptions that underlie all population projections and make them much less than certainties for the future. He cited past instances in which the assumptions underlying the projections were upset by contrary familial behavior (e.g., the baby boom of the late 'forties and the 'fifties, which followed the low fertility rates of the 'thirties) and offered also current demographic outlooks which differed from those of our Moskowitz lecturers, e.g. Judith Blake. And he was much taken by Richard Easterlin's "relative income" hypothesis, which relates birth rates to the relationship between current and expected (i.e., desired) standards of living. Professor Kurnow also directed attention to problems associated with the composition of the population, concentrating in that connection on the dependency ratio. He expressed concern that the overall dependency ratio, which Cohen and Westoff described as declining, could still offer serious problems related to the "composition of the dependency class." He called finally for a set of alternative scenarios that would provide the basis for the development of alternative policies.

Professor Wrong was somewhat less critical of the thrust of Dean Cohen's and Professor Westoff's essays than was Professor Kurnow, expressing general agreement with them. However, he shared, to some degree, Kurnow's concern over the complexity of factors affecting fertility rates and was not certain about current population projections becoming future reality, even though he thought it likely. In that connection, he took particular notice of the difference in attitudes toward a declining birth rate in the 'thirties and today. Then, the prospect of a stable population was viewed with alarm as a powerfully negative economic factor. Today, it is generally viewed as a positive factor contributing to a better environmental situation and an improved quality of life.

I express appreciation for the excellent handling of all arrangements for the lectures, as well as for the editorial preparation of this volume. Most particularly thanks go to Susan Greenbaum, and also to Virginia Moress. I appreciate also the work of the staff of The Free Press for the efficiency with which they moved the manuscript through to final publication.

Abraham L. Gitlow, Dean
College of Business and
Public Administration
New York University

March 16, 1977

THE CHARLES C. MOSKOWITZ
MEMORIAL LECTURES

THE CHARLES C. MOSKOWITZ MEMORIAL LECTURES were established through the generosity of a distinguished alumnus of the College of Business and Public Administration, Mr. Charles C. Moskowitz of the Class of 1914, who retired after many years as Vice President-Treasurer and a Director of Loew's Inc.

In establishing these lectures, it was Mr. Moskowitz's aim to contribute to the understanding of the function of business and its underlying disciplines in society by providing a public forum for the dissemination of enlightened business theories and practices.

The College of Business and Public Administration and New York University are deeply grateful to Mr. Moskowitz for his continued interest in, and contribution to, the educational and public service program of his alma mater.

This volume is the eighteenth in the Moskowitz series. The earlier ones, published by New York University Press, are:

February, 1961   *Business Survival in the Sixties*
Thomas F. Patton, President and Chief Executive Officer
Republic Steel Corporation

November, 1961   *The Challenges Facing Management*
Don G. Mitchell, President
General Telephone and Electronics Corporation

November, 1962   *Competitive Private Enterprise Under Government Regulation*
Malcolm A. MacIntyre, President
Eastern Air Lines

November, 1963   *The Common Market: Friend or Competitor?*
Jesse W. Markham, Professor of Economics, Princeton University
Charles E. Fiero, Vice President, The Chase Manhattan Bank
Howard S. Piquet, Senior Specialist in International Economics, Legislative Reference Service, The Library of Congress

November, 1964   *The Forces Influencing the American Economy*
Jules Backman, Research Professor of Economics, New York University
Martin R. Gainsbrugh, Chief Economist and Vice President, National Industrial Conference Board

November, 1965 *The American Market of the Future*
   Arno H. Johnson, Vice President and Senior Economist, J. Walter Thompson Company
   Gilbert E. Jones, President, IBM World Trade Corporation
   Darrell B. Lucas, Professor of Marketing and Chairman of the Department, New York University

November, 1966 *Government Wage-Price Guideposts in the American Economy*
   George Meany, President, American Federation of Labor and Congress of Industrial Organizations
   Roger M. Blough, Chairman of the Board and Chief Executive Officer, United States Steel Corporation
   Neil H. Jacoby, Dean, Graduate School of Business Administration, University of California at Los Angeles

November, 1967 *The Defense Sector in the American Economy*
   Jacob K. Javits, United States Senator, New York
   Charles J. Hitch, President, University of California
   Arthur F. Burns, Chairman, Federal Reserve Board

November, 1968 *The Urban Environment: How It Can Be Improved*

William E. Zisch, Vice-chairman of the Board, Aerojet-General Corporation

Paul H. Douglas, Chairman, National Commission on Urban Problems

Professor of Economics, New School for Social Research

Robert C. Weaver, President, Bernard M. Baruch College of the City University of New York

Former Secretary of Housing and Urban Development

November, 1969   *Inflation: The Problems It Creates and the Policies It Requires*

Arthur M. Okun, Senior Fellow, The Brookings Institution

Henry H. Fowler, General Partner, Goldman, Sachs & Co.

Milton Gilbert, Economic Adviser, Bank for International Settlements

March, 1971   *The Economics of Pollution*

Kenneth E. Boulding, Professor of Economics, University of Colorado

Elvis J. Stahr, President, National Audubon Society

Solomon Fabricant, Professor of Economics, New York University

Former Director, National Bureau of Economic Research

Martin R. Gainsbrugh, Adjunct Professor of Economics, New York University

Chief Economist, National Industrial
Conference Board

April, 1971   *Young America in the NOW World*
Hubert H. Humphrey, Senator from
Minnesota
Former Vice President of the United
States

April, 1972   *Optimum Social Welfare and Productivity: A Comparative View*
Jan Tinbergen, Professor of Development Planning, Netherlands School
of Economics
Abram Bergson, George F. Baker
Professor of Economics, Harvard
University
Fritz Machlup, Professor of Economics, New York University
Oskar Morgenstern, Professor of
Economics, New York University

April, 1973   *Fiscal Responsibility: Tax Increases
or Spending Cuts?*
Paul McCracken, Edmund Ezra Day
University, Professor of Business
Administration, University of
Michigan
Murray L. Weidenbaum, Edward
Mallinckrodt Distinguished University Professor, Washington University
Lawrence S. Ritter, Professor of Finance, New York University

Robert A. Kavesh, Professor of Finance, New York University

March, 1974   *Wall Street in Transition: The Emerging System and Its Impact on the Economy*

Henry G. Manne, Distinguished Professor of Law, Director of the Center for Studies in Law and Economics, University of Miami Law School

Ezra Solomon, Dean Witter Professor of Finance, Stanford University

March, 1975   *Leaders and Followers in an Age of Ambiguity*

George P. Shultz, Professor, Graduate School of Business, Stanford University

President, Bechtel Corporation

March, 1976   *The Economic System in an Age of Discontinuity: Long-Range Planning or Market Reliance?*

Wassily Leontief, Nobel Laureate, Professor of Economics, New York University

Herbert Stein, A. Willis Robertson Professor of Economics, University of Virginia

Previous volumes of The Charles C. Moskowitz Memorial Lectures are published by New York University Press, 21 West Fourth Street, New York, N.Y. 10003.

CONTENTS

IMPLICATIONS OF POPULATION GROWTH IN THE UNITED STATES: ECONOMIC, SOCIAL, AND POLITICAL IMPLICATIONS

Wilbur J. Cohen
Dean, School of Education
The University of Michigan

The implications of population growth in the United States is indeed a subject with such wide ramifications that this paper will raise many more questions than it answers. The full significance of the topic becomes more complex as other socio-economic developments that are interrelated are also considered. Among the most important of these are: productivity and economic growth, prices, wages, savings, and income distribution; employment, family, leisure and childrearing patterns; the redistribution of population within the nation; the more effective utilization of the skills of women, minorities, and the disadvantaged; the impact of energy and environmental costs and controls and their potential effect on the nature of family life, employment, and other conditions.

Population growth and population policy must be viewed as an important element in relation to other variable forces in our national life. The increased concern in recent years about the quality of life is changing the character of our public discussions about population policy and related developments. There is frequent repetition in the public press of the belief that more is not better, but it is also true that less is not better either. Nor is the continuation of the same necessarily better.

The major change that has taken place in the last ten to fifteen years in connection with quantitative studies related to population and economic policy is that they are now being viewed in relation to *quality* and to changes in life-style, as well. What we include in the quality of life[1] will differ with different persons. And what we include in life-styles will also differ with time and place. But discussions of population policy must take into account many subjective elements that are difficult to define, measure, and predict but are, nevertheless, significant, real, and of growing importance to more people.

In 1968 I was Chairman of the President's Committee on Population and Family Planning. Our report issued on November 18, 1968, contained a number of recommendations which have now been adopted. However, there is one recommendation that has not received the attention I believe it deserves: "That the Office of Education provides significant assistance to appropriate education agencies in the development of materials on population and family life."[2]

In our explanation of this recommendation we stated:

"All levels of the educational system stand in need of materials and curricula on the causes and consequences of population change, so that the American people can confront population issues intelligently. Also needed are curricula on family life so that personal decisions about marriage and parenthood can be made responsibly and with adequate information."

I continue to support this recommendation. The increase in our urban population and the changes in the economy have had a serious impact on family life. During the recent Presidential campaign, the Democratic candidate, Mr. Carter, assigned Mr. Joseph Califano, the present Secretary of Health, Education, and Welfare, to make a study of the pressures affecting the American family. His report made in September 1976 summarized a number of significant changes taking place that affect the family:

—A dramatic increase in the proportion of mothers working outside the home, which now includes over one third of mothers with preschool children, and one half of mothers with school-age children, proportions which have more than doubled in the last 25 years.

—An increase in the divorce rate to the point where two out of every five marriages in the United States end in divorce, with an even higher percentage of teenage marriages resulting in divorce.

—An increase in births out of wedlock. In 1960 one of every 20 women giving birth was not married; today, it is about one in eight.

—More than 600,000 children continue to be

born each year to teenage mothers and these children have a higher-than-average risk of birth defects.

—The virtual extinction of extended families. In 1900, for example, 50 percent of the households in Boston consisted of children, parents, and at least one other adult relative; the comparable figure today is four percent.

—Residential mobility rates which reveal that the average American moves 14 times in his or her lifetime and 20 percent of our population moves each year.

—A new family member has appeared: television. The average child by age 16 now spends more hours watching TV than attending school, and the average child between ages 5 and 15 views the killing of over 13,000 persons on television.[3]

Two current developments may be noted growing out of the consideration of these many factors: (1) the interest in requiring a "family impact analysis" in connection with policies, proposals, and legislation advanced by public bodies similar to the requirement about environmental impact statements required of federal agencies;[4] and (2) the interest in articulating a national policy on families to be spelled out for the guidance of individuals and public and private agencies.

Both developments involve difficult problems. Not only as to what is meant by a family but also what exactly is beneficial, hurtful, or even neutral to different kinds of families. How do we define and identify the strengths and weaknesses of different kinds of families? At the beginning of this century there was a strong emphasis on the homogenization and Americanization of the child and family. This had many constructive results in unifying our national consciousness. Today there is a growing emphasis on the pride and differences in minority and ethnic families which the members of such families say should be preserved and encouraged.

Other questions that need consideration are: Should single-parent families be discouraged, accepted, or provided with special help through the tax and social service systems? Should three-generational families be encouraged and helped? If so, how?

Population Estimates

The Bureau of the Census has developed three projections of the population of the United States to the year 2050.[5] They result in widely different overall results, depending upon different assumptions about future fertility. I have chosen, however, to utilize a specific population estimate for discussion purposes in order to discuss several likely trends.

The Social Security Administration makes a single population projection for the purpose of estimating future costs of the social security program. An estimate made in 1974 and published in 1975 assumes that fertility rates will slowly increase to 2.1 children per woman in the year 2005 and then remain level from 2005 to 2050, and that mortality rates will decline about 15 percent from 1970 to 2050. This projection results in a population of about 300 million by the years 2035–2040, with about 80 million children and youth under age 20, about 170 million persons in the productive age group between ages 20 and 64, and about 50 million persons age 65 and over.[6] (See Appendix for tabular material.)

These projections for the year 2040 result in an aged group of about 17 percent of the total population compared to a little over 10 percent at the present time and a child and youth population of about 27 percent compared to about 36 percent at the present time (1974).[7]

These two aspects of population growth during the next 75 years warrant special consideration. They are (1) the likelihood that the number of children and youth very likely will be a smaller proportion of the total population, and (2) the virtual certainty that older persons will be a much larger proportion of the total population.

These two developments are likely to bring significant modifications in our institutions and attitudes.

In considering policies and prospects evolving from these demographic changes, we must also take into account a number of related changes which are also taking place. Some of the most obvious are: the prospects for continuation of lower fertility rates and the reduction in the number of larger families; the wider acceptance of divorce and remarriage, with children growing up in more than one family; the widespread use of the contraceptive pill and its still unknown effect on the future health of mothers and children; the wider acceptance of abortion and its impact on marriage, while at the same time there is evidence of a substantial number of teen-age pregnancies, low-birth-weight babies, and children born out of wedlock; increased employment of women with children; the existence of more than 10 million children on the welfare rolls; the acceptance of single-parent families; intermarriage of partners from different religious, racial, and ethnic groups; and the lack of employment opportunities for young people.

This is only a partial list of factors affecting the future of our society.

Decline in the Proportion of Children

There are many possible implications of a decline in the proportion of children in the population. Combined with an increase in the proportion of the aged, the impact may be especially important on our political institutions. Will they result in a more conservative political philosophy? Will innovation and experimentation be less acceptable? Will the rate of scientific and technological change be slower? Will the result be a kind of "demographic stagnation," which Alfred Sauvy, the French demographer, indicates may result in a "population of old people ruminating over old ideas in old houses"?[8]

We cannot answer these questions in any simple manner. But we must be aware of the potentially profound effect these developments may have on our nation.

The decrease in the proportion of children and youth in the population and the recent decline in the number of births have already had the effect of cutting back on the numbers of teachers produced by schools of education. Teaching has long been a very important area of academic concentration and job opportunity for women. The so-called surplus of teachers may well result in women's competing with men for jobs in business, government, and labor more than before. The emphasis on affirmative action programs in employment and education may open more higher paid and more influential positions for women and restrict the monopoly men have had in the decision-making roles in the economy and political system. On the other hand, it may serve to introduce more stress in women's lives, and this stress and competition may alter both men's and women's life-styles in the future. To what extent this will produce beneficial and adverse effects we can only wait and see.

With regard to teachers, it may be possible that we can shift our emphasis on improving the *quality* of teachers and teaching in the years ahead. This is not an easy task. But there is at present a great deal of attention to competency-based evaluation of teachers. I believe that with more collective bargaining in education and the presence of more male teachers in elementary and secondary education we may be able to develop, retain, and encourage a wider range of individuals and abilities in our K–12 education system.

The continued reliance, however, in most states on the property tax as a major source of financing K–12 education presents a real political and community problem. It is not so much that the property tax is a grossly inequitable tax but rather that its clear and immediate effect on both young and old persons acts as a convenient psychological and political opportunity to protest taxes in general. I doubt that the property tax can be retained as a major source of financing education as the number and proportion of the aged increases.

The continued increase in employment of women with young children is likely to serve to expand the need for day care for children and early childhood development centers. This would increase the employment opportunities for women in this area. But much depends on how these services for young children will be organized and delivered. Will they become part of the public education system or part of the services provided in the factory or business in which the parent works? Will the private sector take on a major responsibility for such activities? And how will they be financed? These questions have set in motion a series of debatable issues that are likely to precipitate a political controversy as they did in 1971, when President Nixon vetoed the Mondale–Brademas child care bill.[9]

A possible line of action that may evolve is that the federal government over the next several years may assume a larger portion of state and local costs of welfare and Medicaid. The commitment by President Carter for welfare reform and national health insurance may lead in this direction. If so, welfare reform and national health insurance may be the most significant federal aid to education program to evolve during the coming decade.

The Aged

The increased number of older persons raises questions about the ability of the economy in the long run to finance the cost of an acceptable retirement program for a larger proportion of the population. A great deal will depend upon the future growth rate of the economy, the retirement age, and the level of payments or what is usually referred to as the "replacement rate" (i.e., the relationship of benefits to prior earnings).

An increasing number of older persons should require and encourage an increase in total savings among younger persons for their retirement. The balance between consumption expenditures and savings has an important effect on the economy. We are not quite sure what the appropriate relationship should be currently to ensure a healthy economy. We are also not sure what it should be for the future to ensure the economic growth necessary to meet the commitments for a larger retired population. But we can be certain we need to keep the relationship continually in mind as the internal composition of our population changes.

We probably shall have to depend more in the future on private pensions and individual investments than we have in the past. Social security must continue to be an important floor of protection but must be supplemented by private savings from a variety of sources. What the effect of this will be is uncertain.[10]

Our current system for providing for the income of the aged is still in the process of development. We need to re-examine the various parts periodically.

The social security system is now in a precarious financial condition as a result of the combined impact of the economic recession and inflation. The inflation increased benefit expenditures at the very time when the recession reduced the expected income to the system. Whatever the cause and whatever the remedy, we must take immediate steps to restore the financial integrity of the social security system. There is both a short-run and a longer-run problem. The short-run problem needs attention immediately.

There are 33 million persons currently drawing benefits under the social security program. There are 100 million persons contributing to the program each year. Unless we take action this year or next, the disability insurance part of the social security system will exhaust its resources.

The indexing of the social security program in 1972 at the recommendation of President Nixon and over the opposition of the House Committee on Ways and Means not only came at an unfortunate and unusual period in economic developments but was marked by an unintentional error in drafting the law. A "double-indexing" factor was erroneously incorporated in the law with respect to future benefits, and this should be repealed.[11]

I believe the social security system would have been in a better situation today with respect to both finances and benefits if the indexing amendments had not been enacted in 1972. I believe Congress would have responded to the inflation and recession needs on an ad hoc basis in a much more satisfactory manner than the automatic provisions did. The experience makes me cautious for the future in relying on automatic provisions which cannot take unexpected economic developments into account satisfactorily.

There are four general sources for raising additional funds for social security:

1. an increase in the tax rate on employers, employees, or both, and the self-employed

2. an increase in the maximum earnings base upon which contributions and benefits are based

3. use of general federal revenues, or an earmarked personal income tax, corporation tax, or value added tax

4. some combination of the other three methods.

The most uncertain element in any examination of the implications of population growth and change in the future is the rate and stability of economic growth. The tremendous improvements in the standard of living during the past 75 years have been achieved by the interaction of population growth and economic growth. But with the increasing cost of energy, the shortages and the exhaustion of key resources, and the concern over impairment of the environment, it is uncertain whether we will be able to continue to meet the expectations of a larger and older population without a number of important changes affecting our economic, political, community, and family structures.

The essence of any reasonably acceptable plan for meeting the expectations of older persons is a satisfactory social compact between older and younger persons. That is essentially what a pension plan aims to do. It is an intergenerational contract or compact that requires younger persons to restrict their current consumption in order that older persons can have assurance of continuity of consumption when they no longer work.

Longer-Range Retirement Policies

One of the most complex and far-reaching social policy issues growing out of an increased aged population is what should be done about longer-range retirement policies. This big and broad issue has these specific problems.

1. Should mandatory retirement by employers be prohibited by law? If so, at or before what age—65, 67, 68, 70, or 72?

2. Should the normal retirement age for full benefits in social security be raised from 65 to some other age? 67, 68, 70?

3. Should individuals be permitted to retire and draw a reduced benefit from social security before age 62? at age 60?

4. Should the so-called retirement test in social security ($3,000 in 1977) be repealed or liberalized so that more older persons who work can also draw social security benefits?

5. Should the present "replacement rate" of social security benefits (approximately 50 percent of earnings at the maximum earnings amount, for a husband and wife) be reduced in order to lower the long-run costs of social security as wages rise and thus provide a larger role for private savings?

Under the existing Social Security Act the Secretary of Health, Education, and Welfare is required to appoint an Advisory Council on Social Security every four years to make findings and recommendations on the social security system.[12] It is expected that such a Council will be appointed by Secretary Califano in the near future, and some of the basic issues will be examined.

The previous Advisory Council (1975) made a preliminary stab at some of these issues, but the divergence of views and the unrepresentative selection of the labor members of the Council has not resulted in the general utilization or acceptance of their report. They nevertheless did discuss a number of very important issues and proposals.

With respect to the retirement age under social security, the following observation was made:

> The Council recognizes that under current demographic projections there will be a sharp rise in the number of people who will have reached retirement age relative to the working age population in the first several decades of the next century. Although the Council is not recommending an increase in the age of eligibility for social security retirement benefits, the Council does believe that such a change might merit consideration in the next century, when the financial burden of social security taxes on people still working may become excessive.[13]

The Subcommittee on Finance of the Council reported to the Council a suggestion "that every six months the retirement age be increased by one month, beginning in 2005 and ending in 2023. In the latter year, then, the retirement age would have been increased to 68, and the 'early' retirement age increased to 65.'' The Subcommittee reported that this proposal would decrease the combined contribution rate for the system from 16.1 percent to 14.6 percent for the period 2025–50.[14]

Dependency Ratios

A more appropriate way of looking at the longer-range implications of our population growth is to break down the population into three broad age groups: children and youth under the age of 20; persons in the productive age group, 20–64; and older persons, age 65 and over. We can relate the children and aged—the "dependent" groups—to the "productive" age group and thus obtain a general measure of the "dependency" ratio in our population.

In 1973 the child dependency ratio was 67.5, the aged, 18.6—for a total of 86.1. As the fertility rate declines or remains low, the child dependency ratio drops during the next 75 years to about 50, while the aged dependency ratio rises to 25 to 30.[15]

The dependency ratio was about 90 during the period 1960–70. Utilizing the Social Security Administration estimates, the dependency ratio is estimated to fall to about 65 in the year 2010 and reach a high of 80 in 2030—a figure still below the 1960 level.

Thus, the overall dependency ratio is expected to decline in the future. If that occurs, the financial problem of meeting the retirement income of the aged for the persons in the productive age groups does not seem as formidable as it appears by itself in view of the reduction in costs in raising children.

I also believe that there will continue to be real economic growth in the United States in the years immediately ahead. Consequently, during the next 25 years we shall have both population and economic growth but, in my opinion, both probably at a much slower rate than in the past 76 years.[16]

This slower rate of growth will bring with it many significant adjustments. But I do not believe it will or should result in a steady-state economic or social system. The consequences of energy shortage and pollution (air, water, noise, urban slums, and nuclear waste) are very serious and must be given high priority. The problems of energy, pollution, and the decay of the inner cities are all closely interlocked with population policies. While magnitudes are of major importance for economic, social, and political analyses, more attention can and should be given in the future to policies relating to the *distribution, quality,* and *creativity* of the population. In brief, we should develop policies that will uncrowd our congested cities, rely less on the individual automobile for transportation, and consider carefully the impact of all these changes on the family and the community.

Viewed from an overall national perspective, the cost of both retirement payments and medical care for the older population as a group will increase not only in dollars but as a percentage of the gross national product. If more individuals retire at an earlier age, and if more older persons survive with chronic disabilities, the overall cost could be substantial and could be considered burdensome by business and younger people who will be contributing to meet the cost.

Of course, many younger persons would prefer to have the current contributions assigned to a pension, retirement, or social security program available to them for current consumption. If the contributions for retirement continue to increase, as I think they will under both public and private plans, then we must have a much better program of education about the wisdom of paying the costs and saving for the future than we do at the present time. I would hope that the private and public sectors would work together in a common effort in this educational endeavor since they have a common concern in this area.

The Life Expectancy of Women and Health Costs

The increase in the life expectancy of both men and women over the past 75 years is a generally recognized fact, and the implications are also widely recognized. Another aspect of this development warrants further study and attention as to its future implications. This is the continuing increase in the difference between the life expectancies of men and women.

In 1900 the difference between the life expectancy at birth of men and women was about one year. By 1960 the difference had increased to 6.7 years, by 1973 to 7.7 years.

This important development also can be stated in other ways: Life expectancy at age 65 in 1973 was 13.2 years for men and 17.3 years for women—a four-year difference. The proportion of men surviving to age 65 was 67.5 percent, compared to 82.2 percent for women. The median age at death was 72 for men and nearly 80 for women.[17]

These developments will have special significance not only for retirement income policies but also for health and medical care and the costs of providing such services.

If these trends continue, the costs of medical services are most likely to rise because of the higher cost of medical services for older people. The Bureau of the Census and the Social Security Administration projections both assume that the differential between the life expectancy at birth of women and men will increase to 8.1 years (i.e., 69.9 and 78.0) ultimately.[18]

Health Expenditures Vary Widely by Age

Per capita health expenditures vary widely by age. In 1975, per capita personal health expenditures were $212 for persons under age 19, $472 for persons age 19–64, and $1,360 for persons age 65 and over. The per capita expenditure for persons of all ages was $476.[19]

The per capita cost of personal health services

for the aged was more than six times that for children and youth!

The 10 percent of the population who were aged utilized 30 percent of all personal health expenditures, while the 25 percent of the population who were children and youth used only 15 percent of the total. There was, in effect, a redistribution of health and medical expenditures of about 20 percent of the total transferred from children and youth to the aged.

Since the relationship of per capita health and medical expenditures for the aged is about three times that of the entire population ($1360 to $476) and about three times the proportion of expenditures in relation to the proportion of the population (30 percent to 10 percent), we may speculate that if, and when, the aged population reaches about 17 percent, and unless there is some very significant reduction in the utilization or cost of health and medical services by the aged, about one half of all personal health expenditures in the nation might be expended on the aged! Another way of putting it is that the total cost of health and medical services might represent about 12 to 15 percent of the gross national product, compared to 8.6 percent in 1976!

Concluding Observations

The major social policy issue that derives from population changes in my opinion is how as a nation can we fulfill our commitment to provide a more satisfactory level of living to an increasing number of aged persons, improving the health and education of our children and youth, and also providing additional income to the working population as an incentive and reward for their production and contribution. To provide an improved health and education system and a higher level of income to the young, the old, and the middle-aged will take a more conscious, deliberate, and selective set of economic and social policies than we have had previously.

I believe we must expand, extend, strengthen, and improve our health, educational, and social services to improve the quality of our population and the quality of life for the present and future members of our society. I support appropriate and well-considered proposals for federal action in these areas. But I believe that this cannot be accomplished by public or private funds or agencies alone or in combination without strengthening the basic role of the mother, father, and family, including grandparents.

We have too many forces at work in our society that undermine the role of the family. During the past several years there has been much criticism against the errors, misjudgments, and mistakes of the federal government. Some of these criticisms are well founded. But state and local governments have also failed to carry out their basic responsibilities for the welfare of children and families. They have not adequately met the challenge of crime, drug abuse, delinquency, and education of the young, all of which is their constitutional duty. They appeal to the Federal government for more revenue sharing funds while they are ineffective in remedying the complaints about their failures.

We need a major attack on transforming the public dialogue about these issues from preserving states' rights to remedying states' wrongs. Additional federal funds to the states should be conditional on a step-by-step remedy of state and local inadequacies, inefficiencies, and ineffectiveness. One step might be that within five years each state receiving federal general revenue funds must have a minimum state income tax and must have a metropolitan area system for all services including education and transportation.

The increased cost of energy will undoubtedly intensify the internal migration of population to the sun belt. This is likely to create many new problems in providing services to the people in these areas. It may also result in some longer-run reallocation of political power as the Northern and at present large industrial states lose their heavy electoral college influence to other states. The addition of 50 million to 100 million more people to our population combined with the change in the age, sex, and racial composition indicates the possibility of many changes in the economic, political, and social institutions under which our children and grandchildren will live.

Notes

1. For a discussion of some of these factors see Wilbur J. Cohen, "The Quality of Life and Social Indicators," National Bureau of Economic Research, National Bureau Report Supplement, No. 9, March 1972. A speech given at the NBER Fiftieth An-

niversary Human Capital Colloquim, May 13, 1971.

2. *Population and Family Planning: The Transition from Concern to Action,* Report of the President's Committee on Population and Family Planning (Washington, D.C.: Government Printing Office, November 1968), p. 10.

3. Joseph A. Califano, Jr., "American Families: Trends, Pressures and Recommendations." A Preliminary Report to Governor Jimmy Carter, September 17, 1976, 15 pp. (mimeograph).

4. Sheila B. Kamerman, "Developing a Family Impact Statement," Foundation for Child Development, New York, May 1976, 20 pp. Also "A Program for Training Family Impact Analysts," Minnesota Family Study Center, University of Minnesota, 12 pp. (1976).

5. *Population Estimates and Projections: Projections of the Population of the United States: 1975 to 2050,* Current Population Reports Series P-25, No. 601, October 1975 (Washington, D.C.: Government Printing Office, U.S. Bureau of the Census, 1975). 143 pp.

6. *1975 Annual Report of the Board of Trustees of the Federal Old-Age and Survivors Insurance and Disability Insurance Trust Funds,* May 6, 1975, House Document No. 94-135, 94th Congress, 1st Session, House Committee on Ways and Means (Washington, D.C.: Government Printing Office, 1975), 58 pp., pp. 47–48.

7. Data for 1974 obtained from *Population Estimates* (note 5, above), pp. 10 and 40.

8. Robert Reinhold, "New Population Trends Transforming U.S.," *New York Times,* Sunday, February 6, 1977, pp. 1 and 42.

9. For a summary of President Nixon's objections and Congressional rebuttal, see House of Representatives Report No. 92-1570, "Comprehensive Child Development Act" to accompany H.R. 6748, October 11, 1972, 92d Congress, 2d Session.

10. The reserve funds built up in private pension plans totaled $192 billion at the end of 1974. (The reserves probably reached about $225 billion by the end of 1976.) Total contributions to these plans in 1974 were $25 billion, of which $23 billion came from employers and $2 billion from employees. These totals exclude pension plans for federal, state, and local governmental employees as well as pension plans for the self-employed. Alfred Skolnik, "Private Pension Plans, 1950–74," *Social Security Bulletin*, June 1976, p. 4. The excess of contributions over benefits which went to build up reserves was about $12 billion in 1974.

11. For discussions of the "decoupling" proposals of "double-indexing," see *Report of the Panel on Social Security Financing to the Committee on Finance*, United States Senate, February 1975, 31 pp., and *Report of the Consultant Panel on Social Security to the Congressional Research Service*, August 1976, 119 pp.

12. Section 706 of the Social Security Act.

13. *Reports of the Quadrennial Advisory Council on Social Security*, House Document No. 94-75, March 10, 1975, House Committee on Ways and Means, 179 pp., p. XVII.

14. *Ibid.*, p. 118.

15. "Maternal and Child Health Care Act," Hearings before the Subcommittee on Health and the Environment of the House Committee on Interstate and Foreign Commerce, 94th Cong., Second Session

on H.R. 12937 and H.R. 14309, June 16, 1976, p. 132.

16. The average annual compounded rates of economic growth from 1910 to 1969 were 3.1 percent and from 1935 to 1969, 4.4 percent. The per capita growth rates for different periods from 1913 to 1967 varied from 1.5 percent for 1950–60 to 3.3 percent for 1960–67. An annual average per capita growth rate of about 2 percent for the future is a real possibility depending upon the availability of energy and other resources. *Statistical Abstract of the United States, 1970,* U.S. Dept. of Commerce, 1970, Tables 474 and 475, pp. 313–314.

17. *Vital Statistics of the United States, 1973,* Life Tables, Vol. II, Section 5 (Washington, D.C.: U.S. DHEW, Public Health Service, National Center for Health Statistics, 1975), p. 5–4.

18. *Population Estimates* (note 5, above), p. 26.

19. Marjorie Smith Mueller and Robert M. Gibson, "Age Differences in Health Care Spending, Fiscal Year 1975," *Social Security Bulletin,* June 1976, pp. 18–31. Personal health expenditures in the fiscal year 1975 were $103.2 billion. Together with all other health expenditures (research, construction, etc.), total national health expenditures were $118.5 billion in 1975 (p. 18).

Appendix: Population Projections, 1985–2050

A projection was made of the United States population (including persons overseas covered by the old-age, survivors, and disability insurance program) for future quinquennial years, by 5-year age

Projections of the U.S. Population by Broad Groups, 1985–2050

	Population (in thousands) as of July 1				65 and over as—	
Year	Under 20	20 to 64	65 and over	Total	Percent of total	Ratio of 20 to 64
1985	70,754	141,512	26,741	239,006	11.2	0.189
1990	71,929	147,457	28,789	248,176	11.6	.195
1995	74,264	152,261	30,015	256,540	11.7	.197
2000	76,333	157,038	30,214	263,585	11.5	.192
2005	76,349	162,970	30,580	269,898	11.3	.188
2010	76,222	167,432	32,662	276,316	11.8	.195
2015	76,990	168,840	36,917	282,747	13.1	.219
2020	78,561	167,873	42,061	288,494	14.6	.251
2025	80,030	165,608	47,448	293,087	16.2	.287
2030	80,768	164,636	51,227	296,632	17.3	.311
2035	81,202	166,502	51,879	299,583	17.3	.312
2040	81,989	169,501	50,806	302,296	16.8	.300
2045	83,213	172,462	49,257	304,931	16.2	.286
2050	84,462	173,843	49,352	307,657	16.0	.284

Source: *1975 Annual Report of the Board of Trustees of the Federal Old-Age and Survivors Insurance and Disability Insurance Trust Funds,* May 6, 1975, House Document No. 94-135, 94th Congress, 1st Session, House Committee on Ways and Means (Washington, D.C.: Government Printing Office, 1975).

groups and by sex. The starting point was the population on July 1, 1973, as estimated by the Bureau of the Census from the 1970 Census and from births, deaths, and migration in 1970–73. This population estimate was adjusted for differences in the geographical areas covered by the estimate of the Bureau of the Census and those covered by the old-age, survivors, and disability insurance system.

In the population projection it was assumed that through 2050 mortality rates will continue the general trends established over the 1950–1970 period. This results in an overall reduction in mortality rates of about 15 percent from 1970 to 2050.

The total fertility rate was assumed to decrease from its current level to a level of 1.7 children per woman in fiscal year 1977 and then slowly increase to an ultimate level of 2.1 children per woman in fiscal year 2005. It was assumed to remain level at 2.1 from 2005 to 2050. The 2.1 ultimate total fertility rate is close to the population replacement rate and would ultimately result in close-to-zero population growth. In addition, the projection assumed a small amount of net immigration.

FERTILITY DECLINE IN THE UNITED STATES AND ITS IMPLICATIONS

Charles F. Westoff
Director, Office of Population Research
Princeton University

The Decline of Fertility

Every few months, when the birthrate records a new low, I receive telephone calls from journalists and radio and television commentators asking me for *the* explanation. The question is sometimes formulated in terms of what explains this particular decline—as if some specific events occurred which were responsible—but more often it is a more general inquiry about why has American fertility been declining in the past few years. They want to know whether it is because of the pill, or the greater availability of abortion, or the recent recession, or women's lib, or some new attitudes of the younger generation. I have finally formulated a stock answer, which is that this is the wrong question to ask. The more interesting question, and one that experts do not wholly understand, is why fertility went *up* during the baby boom of the 'fifties. After all, we have evidence that fertility rates in the United States had been declining fairly steadily for two centuries. The one major interruption of that decline was the baby boom, which lasted in this country and a few others (Canada, Australia, New Zealand) for about a decade. The decline that has occurred since 1960 can most sensibly be regarded as a resumption of a long-term historical downward trend of fertility. Moreover, that historical decline, although it began in the United States earlier than in most other countries, is hardly a uniquely American phenomenon. That decline has been occurring in France for as long and in other industrialized countries since about 1870. The evidence from the recent postwar period shows striking similarities. Just two years ago I had the assignment of reviewing the demographic situations in the developed nations of the world, and I observed a dramatic convergence of fertility. In most of those countries, perhaps now 26 of the 33, fertility rates are at or below the replacement level of 2.1 births per woman. And these countries vary considerably in their political systems, their economic conditions, and the methods of fertility control available. What most commonly passes for population policy in the industrialized countries, in vivid contrast to the developing countries, is pronatalist in character, involving maternal and child benefits and various financial incentives for family formation. Little demographic impact of such policies has been evident, with the possible exception of some East European countries.

So I have now told my inquiring journalist that

the decline in fertility and the decline in population growth it implies are neither new nor uniquely American. Since there's not much of a story in that response, and since he must salvage something for his editor, he goes on to ask why fertility has been declining for so long, and more interestingly, how long will it continue, how low will it get, and what the implications are of a low growth, or no growth, or even a negative growth rate.

The reasons for the historic decline are numerous, I explain. They include a wide range of fairly obvious social changes that have accompanied the transformation of Western society from a rural setting and an agrarian economy to an increasingly urban and metropolitan setting with a highly industrialized and now increasingly service-oriented economy. These changes include decreasing infant and child mortality, universal education, the decline of religious authority, and the emergence of an ethos of rationality, equality of women, and a pervasive consumer-oriented culture. Such changes have decreased both the traditional imperative of having children and the compatibility of large families with emerging life-styles. When changes of this kind are combined with the development of birth control technology, it is not surprising that a small-family pattern has emerged. How long will it continue and how low will it get? These are more difficult questions, the kind of questions that demographers have hardly shown any great success in answering. In fact, their forecasting record has been rather dismal.

There is no question that the fertility rate in the United States is currently very low. The total fertility rate, which is apparently still declining, is down to the lowest it has ever been in this country, below 1.8 births per woman (projected from current rates to a lifetime total); the birthrate is 14.6 per 1,000 population, and the death rate is 8.9. Were it not for a net legal immigration of about 400,000 per year, the growth rate would be 5.7 per 1,000 population. With immigration included, it is about 8.0 per 1,000 population. Even with continued immigration at that volume, such below-replacement fertility means that the population will stop growing in 50 years at about 250 million and will then begin to decline. If such a rate continued, it would imply a total of 245 million in the year 2000, a far cry from the 300 million anticipated by the President in a message to Congress only eight years ago. But such projections assume the continuation of that rate of fertility. Is fertility likely to rise or decline? The honest answer is that nobody knows; only more or less plausible speculations can be advanced. Back in the late 'thirties there was also a very low fertility level, and some expressions of apprehension about the prospect of impending decline were heard. Such concerns disappeared rapidly with the war and the ensuing baby boom. How do we know that another baby boom is not in store? Only recently some demographers were talking about a second baby boom as a kind of echo effect of the first one, the large number of babies that could be expected as the products of the first baby boom reached the age of parenthood. This has not yet occurred, only because the extremely low fertility rates have outweighed the increase in the numbers of young people.

Some economist-demographers are persuaded that another baby boom will develop as the children born during the recent years of declining birthrates come of age and enter the labor force, where, because of their smaller numbers, they will enjoy a competitive advantage and thus brighter prospects. They are therefore expected to marry earlier and have more children because their incomes will be relatively higher and their futures more promising. The empirical evidence for this is essentially the relationship between the increase in the number of births over time with declining cohort fertility. In more recent years the small cohorts of the 'thirties experienced high fertility in the 'fifties, whereas those born during the baby boom of the 'fifties are experiencing low fertility in the 'seventies. If the cycle is repeated, those born in the 'seventies will produce another baby boom toward the end of the century.

There are several important factors to consider in evaluating this theory and our demographic future in general. One is what appears to be a massive postponement of marriage. A steady decline since 1960 in the proportion of women marrying at ages 20–24 may be the unrecognized beginning of a radical change in the family as we know it. Another factor is the changing status and role of women in our society. The assumption that the future increase in the demand for labor which will result from smaller cohorts entering the labor force will automatically translate into higher fertility ignores the very real changes in women's attitudes toward work (the supply of labor includes female labor also), marriage and childbearing. I shall re-

turn to these subjects at greater length toward the
end of this essay, when I explore the diverse social
implications of declining fertility.

There is also a seemingly irreversible change:
The technology of fertility control has improved
tremendously in the past 15 years and is widely dif-
fused throughout the population. Virtually all
American married couples use contraception if they
are not pregnant, trying to get pregnant, or sterile.
Among those currently using contraception in
1975, three out of four were either sterilized, using
the pill, or using the IUD. Abortion is now widely
available, and further technological developments
in fertility control (e.g., to enable the predeter-
mination of sex of offspring) are on the horizon.
We are fast approaching the perfect contraceptive
society in which unwanted births will become non-
existent, although teenage childbearing continues to
constitute a major social problem.

What fertility can we expect in such a population? For one thing, annual fertility rates should
become more volatile, more responsive to short-
term fluctuations in the economy. But perfect control of fertility does not imply that couples will
want no more than one or two children. In theory,
they could just as easily opt for twice that number.
But larger family size in the future does not seem
likely to me in the light of historical trends, in the
nature of the baby boom, or in the character of the
subsequent decline. The historical trends, as already noted, all point in the downward direction.
The one exception, the baby boom, was created not
by a return to the large families of the nineteenth
century but by a movement away from spin-
sterhood, childless marriage, and the one-child

family, and by a bunching together of births at early ages. Only a minor part of the baby boom can be attributed to increases in the proportions having three or more births. The decline in births that occurred in the 'sixties was almost entirely due to a decrease in the number of unplanned births. The accelerated decline since 1970 no doubt continues this trend but probably includes a reduction in the number of planned births as well. Some observers argue that the low fertility of recent years reflects primarily the postponement of births and that the postponed births will be made up in the next few years. The decline in total expected family size (the number of children that women in surveys say they expect to have) does not substantiate this view, and, although some postponement exists, there is now enough evidence to support the view that "later means fewer." Regardless of whether some of this postponement is made up, low fertility at one level or another seems here to stay. What are its implications for our society?

Implications of Declining Fertility

There are a variety of societal implications of declining fertility and population growth which I will try to summarize under the headings of economic, environmental, political, and social consequences. Most of my observations will be based upon the research findings of the Commission on Population Growth and the American Future, on which I served as Executive Director. This Commission, chaired by John D. Rockefeller 3rd, was established by Congress at the request of then President Nixon and was charged with assessing the prospects for U.S. population growth between 1970 and the year 2000, evaluating the effects of such growth on the environment and natural resources, determining the public sector demands that will be required to deal with the anticipated growth in population, and assessing the impact of population growth on the activities of governments at all levels. The Commission was also charged with evaluating "the various means appropriate to the ethical values and principles of this society by which our Nation can achieve a population level properly suited for its environmental, natural resources, and other needs," a mandate which we interpreted as an invitation to formulate a national population policy but in which, as it turned out later, President Nixon had little interest.

Perhaps the most lasting contribution of the Population Commission was not its policy recommendations, many of which have been ignored, but rather its diagnosis of the consequences of population growth in the United States. The research commissioned to evaluate the magnitude of these impacts focused on a clear-cut question: What differences would it make if our population were to grow at a rate consistent with a lifetime average of approximately two children per woman or if it grew at a rate consistent with three children per woman?

The studies utilized the high and low Census Bureau projections published in 1970. The low fertility assumption envisioned at that time was 2.1 births per woman, the value that would be needed to replace one generation with the next, and which, after the age distribution stabilized in two generations, would bring births into balance with deaths—a zero rate of natural increase. As we have seen, our fertility rate is now at 1.8 births per woman, a dramatic drop from the 2.5 rate experienced in 1970. Thus the studies of the Commission are somewhat understated in their calculated impact or, to put it another way, whatever consequences were expected to differentiate the two- from the three-child fertility rate; as its demographic implications unfold over time, will be realized sooner than expected.

The demographic consequences of these different rates on growth are dramatic: Over a century, the two-child average would yield an ultimate stationary population of 350 million, while the three-child average would yield a still rapidly growing population of nearly one billion.

The Census Bureau's population projections to the year 2000 and, in some instances, to 2020, provided the basis for projecting gross national product, labor force growth, household formation, consumer income, and other characteristics needed for the impact studies. The economic and population projections were used to estimate future per capita income; the utilization of mineral, energy, land, and water resources; generation of pollutants; demand for health, educational, and welfare services; and the demand for the products of particular industries.

Economic Consequences

The belief that population growth is necessary for economic growth has a long and deeply rooted history in our country and can be heard even today.

Although it has been radically tempered by recent environmental concerns, there is undoubtedly a considerable segment of the business community that regards a slowing of population growth as the prelude to a stagnating economy. It is not surprising that the two ideas are connected, given the fact that periods of rapid population growth have been periods of rapid economic growth. But the days of rapid growth of the labor force are drawing to an end. What are the economic implications of slowing population growth?

The basic conclusion reached by the Commission was that the vitality of our national economy is more dependent on nondemographic factors but that the population would be better off economically with the lower than with the higher rate of growth:

> We have looked for, and have not found, any convincing economic argument for continued national population growth. The health of our economy does not depend on it. The vitality of business does not depend on it. The welfare of the average person certainly does not depend on it.

The conclusion was reached primarily because lower birthrates reduce the proportion of children (more than it increases the proportion of the aged) in the population and thereby increase the proportion of the population of working age. As a result of this improvement in the dependency ratio, per capita income may be as much as 15 percent higher under the two-child than under the three-child rate of population growth. Also, with a lower birthrate more women can be expected to participate in the labor force.

Of course, it seems reasonable, other things equal, that a higher rate of population growth, which means a higher labor force growth rate, will eventually mean a higher aggregate GNP, but the more sensible economic goal should be to maximize *per capita* GNP, which would result from the lower rate of growth.

One possible economic liability of declining population growth is that the labor force will age somewhat, and concerns have been expressed that an older labor force will lack the flexibility, imagination, and energy of a younger one. There is no real evidence on this subject yet, in part because these are difficult dimensions to assess.

So far we have talked about the *national* economy as though there are no differences in industry or locale. It is certainly evident that businesses which depend on the baby and youth markets are being or will be affected by diminishing numbers of customers. It is also true that other industries such as those producing goods and services for leisure time activities will benefit from higher per capita incomes. Certain industries that depend on growth, such as the housing and construction industries, will also have to make adjustments, although the increase in discretionary income that can be used on second homes will offset the decline in demand somewhat. But these effects can be foreseen and presumably planned for. Once the number of births for a given year is recorded, there is little difficulty in projecting the future age composition.

The economic implications of population

change are more keenly felt at local levels than they are nationally. But population change in cities and in the country is frequently connected with internal migration and associated changes in the demographic and socio-economic composition of the population. Even with approaching population stabilization, problems of the distribution of population will remain. In our recent concerns about too high a rate of growth, we seem to have overlooked the fact that between 1960 and 1970 half of all the counties and 15 of the 21 largest cities in the United States lost population. There is now emerging evidence that between 1970 and 1975 small towns were experiencing new growth for the first time in modern history. Perhaps we are in for a new redistribution in the continuous shifting of people and economic activity.

Environmental Consequences

As everyone knows, there has been a great increase in concern about environmental problems in the United States during the past decade. In all probability, the interest in national population growth that provided much of the impetus to the creation of the Population Commission can be traced to the environmental concerns of the late 'sixties; the connections between population growth and environmental problems, exaggerated as they might have been, were undoubtedly responsible for the brief surfacing of population as a perceived problem.

The Commission addressed the resource and

environmental issues with the same approach that it employed in the economic area; what implications would a two- or three-child rate of growth have for the utilization of resources and for environmental pollution? The main conolusion of the research for resources was that population growth, within the two- to three-child range investigated, is not likely to cause any serious shortages of mineral resources during the rest of this century. The annual consumption of minerals in the year 2000 was estimated to be only 10 percent more under the three-child assumption; the relative difference in energy demands was estimated to be about the same. The main reason that the difference is so slight is the short time horizon of the projection. After the turn of the century, the implications of the different growth assumptions become greater at an accelerating rate. Moreover, both mineral resource and energy consumption in the short run are much more likely to be determined by public taxing and private pricing adjustments (as we learn each time OPEC has a meeting), conservation policies, and technological changes than by population growth.

Population growth plays a more important role in the next quarter of a century for land and water and for recreational resources. The allocation of scarce water supplies in the Southwestern part of the country is already a difficult political and economic problem. Growing population and economic activity will cause the water shortage to spread eastward and northward. High-quality agricultural land will also become more scarce, and food prices will rise even more with a higher than with a lower rate of population growth, especially with environmental policies that restrict the use of pesticides and chemical fertilizers.

Given the projected increase in income, the pressure on natural recreational resources (national parks and campsites) will continue to grow. Population growth at the lower rate was estimated to imply a demand of 30 percent less than at the higher growth rate, in part because the higher rate also means more younger people who typically use such facilities.

The Commission also explored the implications of population growth for air and water pollution. The principal conclusion again was that government environmental policy, technology, and economic growth will be more important between 1970 and 2000 than population growth, at least as illustrated by the example of hydrocarbon emissions. The longer the time period, of course, the more important the effect of population growth would become. As in our discussion of economic consequences, the influence of population on environmental problems is very much a local matter of concentration of people in space, which has more to do, at least at the moment, with distribution than with national growth rates.

The general conclusion reached about the significance of population growth for the environment is that more rapid growth would intensify the problems and make solutions more difficult, perhaps forcing premature solutions to environmental problems. Higher growth might also mean more need for what seems to be an increasingly regulated and bureaucratic life, arising from the necessity to ration increasingly scarce common property resources. Or, to put the conclusion another way, there are no advantages to further growth, and nothing but increasing costs of growth, as time goes on.

Political Consequences

The likelihood that a growing population increases the need for more regulation of our everyday life may be one of the more unattractive political costs of growth in numbers. A related question is how well democratic government functions with ever increasing numbers of citizens. Our political institutions were designed to govern a much smaller population, and, although our institutions have grown and adapted to changing conditions, there are continuing questions. A recent remanifestation of a type of population question is the renewed concern for changing the presidential elections to reflect the popular vote rather than the electoral college notion. This is just part of a more basic concern with maintaining representativeness at the national level. Since the number of representatives in the House was fixed at 435 in 1910, the average number of citizens represented by a single congressman has increased from 211,000 to 500,000; by the year 2000 this figure will reach between 625,000 and 750,000, depending upon which of the two trajectories population growth follows. Perhaps, in an era of television, instant communications and public opinion polls, there has been no real loss—perhaps there has even been a gain—in the interaction between constituents and their elected representatives. Perhaps we romanticize the past in assuming that face-to-face personal contacts used to be more common. And maybe numbers are less important than other considerations, such as quality of the representatives. But it seems clear that some responsiveness may be lost as numbers increase and a citizen's vote counts for less and less. Some part of the growing alienation that journalists and social scientists are fond of describing, that manifests itself in large numbers of nonparticipants in elections, may result from a declining sense of individual significance caused by the sheer growth of population.

The amount of business that legislators conduct has increased enormously over the history of the Republic. There were a thousand times more bills introduced in the most recent Congress compared with the first one, and 20 times as many committee reports. The Speaker of the House some years ago observed: "Nowadays bills which 30 years ago would have been thrashed out for hours or days go through in ten minutes." Given the increase in assistants and the greatly increased flow and availability of information, this can be viewed, in perhaps major part, as an increase in the productivity of legislators, but it undoubtedly does imply some diminution in the amount of individual reflective judgment brought to bear on issues as the amount delegated to assistants increases.

Population growth also causes increasing pressure on our system of justice. The increase in litigation may be more than proportionately related to population size and probably makes some, though minor, contribution to court congestion and legal delays. Perhaps more important, given the fact that the final arbiter is the Supreme Court, and we can have only one final arbiter, increasing litigation means increasing business for the Court, which inevitably means less time spent per decision and fewer cases accepted. This may imply some lowering of the quality of judicial decisions. As the Commission stated:

> In 1824, when our population was 11 million, Daniel Webster could argue an important case before the Supreme Court for several days. Today, oral arguments are usually limited to one hour or less, and the Court hears only a very small percentage of the several thousand cases that arise through the expanded lower court system and the increasingly popular appeals procedures. The same type of pressure extends to the single supreme court in many states.

As with other implications of growth that we have reviewed, the cessation of population growth will not solve any of these problems; it will only make their solution easier.

In the past, the link between numbers and national security provided a basis for more concern about the size of the population than it does now, although even today we occasionally hear such concerns expressed in France, Argentina, and some other countries. Technological developments, including nuclear weaponry, have obviously reduced dependence upon manpower. Military experts claim that a peacetime active duty force of no more than three million is sufficient to ensure national security. Those three million would be less than six percent of the male population 18 to 45 years old, even with the lower of the two population projections. It seems obvious that military manpower requirements are not affected by any reasonable population growth alternative.

One set of implications that concerned the Commission is the significance of population growth for public sector expenditures in education, health, and welfare. The difference between the two- and three-child projections showed rather dramatic implications for the costs of education that occur because of the considerable difference in the number of children to be educated. Assuming continued improvements in the quality of education, the higher population projection would mean an educational expenditure of 13 percent of GNP, or $400 billion, by the year 2000, compared with 9.7 percent of GNP, or $276 billion with the lower rate of growth. A trade-off between quantity and quality can be used to illustrate the demographic effects in a different way. Assuming that 10 percent of our GNP would be spent on education in the year 2000, the larger population would provide 7 percent of students with a higher quality education while 93 percent would receive the same quality as today's students. The lower projection would permit all students to receive the higher-quality education.

Because the number of older citizens in the year 2000, among whom the demand for health services is greatest, will not be affected by birthrates in the preceding three decades, the costs of health care would be expected to amount only to $1 billion a year more for the higher projection. In the long run, of course, the effects of alternative trajectories of population growth on health care would be enormous.

Welfare costs are also affected more by aggregate population growth in the longer run because of their greater sensitivity to changes in the numbers of the aged since they have the highest poverty rates; only about one-third of poor households include children. Hence a lower birthrate cannot have too much effect, at least in the short run. Again, as in the case of health care but unlike education, the significance of population growth is muted in the short run because of the age effects that are not apparent in the first generation.

Once again, throughout this discussion I have been focusing exclusively on the national level, while it is very evident that many of the population effects on government and public services occur at local levels. The daily services provided by state and local governments in police and fire protection, highways, transportation facilities, and sanitation, as well as education, health, and welfare, are closely tied to the numbers of people and their demographic characteristics. The depopulation of rural areas, especially the loss of persons of productive age, has greatly reduced the tax base and the revenues available for public services disproportionate to the decline of demand for such services. Many of the more affluent states are the recipients of migrants who add to their public service demands. The attraction of the central cities for the poor and for more recent foreign migrants and the simultaneous departure of the middle classes increases public service dependency and erodes the economic base. Even with national population stabilization, such internal and foreign migration streams.

One persistent political problem that interacts with the concentration of population is the fragmented government structures that make the effective governance of metropolitan areas impossible. This widely recognized problem will not be solved easily.

Social Consequences

Much of the speculation about the social consequences of a declining birthrate centers upon the significance of the changes implied for the age distribution of the population. I have already noted that the increasing proportion of persons of labor force age will contribute to a rise in *per capita* income. Actually, the composition of dependents in the population will change also as the decline in the proportion of youth will be partly offset by the increase in the proportion of the aged. The increasing balance of our population who are adults may imply various subtle social consequences, which I shall discuss in a moment, but the most obvious and important change ahead is the sheer increase in the number of persons aged 65 and over. Quite aside from what happens to the birthrate in the next couple of generations, the number of persons expected in this age group will grow from 22 million in 1975 to 31 million by 2000 and to about 50 million a generation later, when zero population growth would be reached (following the Census

Bureau projections from the 1975 fertility rate). If our society is now becoming increasingly preoccupied with the health and economic problems of its aged members, and not doing a very good job at it, one can only imagine the problems that are heading our way as the magnitude of the problem grows. It seems highly likely that their problems will receive higher priority as their number and political power increase.

An important political-economic problem seems to lie ahead in connection with the social security program as the ratio of older persons to persons of working age increases. That ratio will increase by about 50 percent between 1975 and the advent of the stationary population. If an earlier age of retirement becomes institutionalized, the ratio would increase even more. Given the fact that these transfer payments from the young to the old are intrinsically on a pay-as-you-go basis, the relative burden on the young will increase. In order to relieve this burden, growth in real income will be necessary.

The future, of course, may witness some changes in the status of the aged, for example, in connection with retirement age. If their status and power do grow, it may be as much a consequence of their increasing proportion of the population due to declining birthrates as of their increasing number. On the other hand, they may have some competition, because as the ranks of the young diminish in supply, the increased demand may well augment *their* status.

Indeed, if one were assigned the task of designing the demographic blueprint for a meritocracy, one would place great emphasis on a uniform annual number of births in order to eliminate the unfair advantages and disadvantages due to rises and declines in the size of birth cohorts. Persons born in the 'twenties and 'thirties, found it relatively easy to enter college and find jobs in the late 'forties and 'fifties, while those born in the baby boom of 1947–57 encountered greatly increased competition in the late 'sixties and early 'seventies. With uniformity of cohort size, one important source of such inequalities would disappear.

One great advantage of avoiding baby booms and birth dearths is the basis it would provide for planning. Schools are a good example. During the 'fifties, a tremendous shortage of schools and of qualified teachers had to be overcome; in the 'sixties the pressure of the baby boom hit the secondary schools, and in the late 'sixties and early 'seventies the colleges were swamped. In recent years the decline of births that began 15 years ago is making itself felt in the elementary schools and the junior high schools, with the result that schools are being shut down and teachers discharged. Colleges and universities will soon be hit hard, and, as everyone connected with these institutions recognizes, the days of expansion are over.

The baby boom is also being blamed for part of the decline in SAT scores. The basic theory, in what appears to be one significant component of this decline, is that children learn as a direct function of their exposure to adults and as a negative function of their exposure to other children close to their own age. The evidence that connects family size with achievement scores from cross-sectional studies is impressive, and the increase in average birth order and the 12-year drop in the SAT test scores 16 or 17 years later shows a very close fit. Since the birthrate has now been declining for almost this long, the theory calls for a halt to this score decline and a reversal in the near future. (Evidence from testing in some secondary schools lends support to this expectation.)

Similarly, some part of the high unemployment rates we have experienced in the past several years is due to the pressures on the job market created by young people entering the labor force for the first time who were the products of the enlarged cohorts of the baby boom. This pressure should begin to ease in the years ahead as the products of the declining birthrate years reach working age, and in another 15 years, as the smaller cohorts of the 'seventies reach working age, there will probably be problems of labor shortages as we now hear about in countries like Japan and in various European nations.

The implication of a constant number of births (equal to the number of deaths) is that the number of persons at each age up to about 50 is very similar. In a stationary population, we will have well over 90 percent as many 50-year-olds as 20-year-olds in contrast to a ratio of about 60 percent today. Since the labor force would have stopped growing in a stationary population, some concerns have been expressed that the relatively larger number of older persons occupying the higher-status positions because of seniority would block the chances of younger persons for advancement and thus reduce the fluidity and mobility in the system. Of course,

earlier age of retirement could influence this potential problem of a stationary population, but this
solution could conflict with the demands of older
persons for the prolongation of working life. Some
observers have even suggested that a stationary
population means an overall reduction in the rate of
social mobility. The demography of a stationary
population is certainly not inconsistent with this
view, but there are so many other factors that determine mobility in a social system (notably the rate
of economic growth, technological change, social
values, personnel policies, etc.) that the role played
by age composition may be very slight by compari-
son.

The same reservations apply to the related
question of whether a stationary population and an
older age composition mean that the rate of social
change will diminish. It might be expected that, as
growth ceases and a more conservative set of attitudes usually associated with older persons begins
to dominate, the rate of social innovation may diminish. (Of course, some of us middle-aged professors who experienced the excesses of students in
the late 'sixties may not find the aging of the population too intolerable.) Part of the association of
conservatism with age may in fact reflect genera-
tional differences in education, although it is reasonable to assume that age is also associated with
increasing equity; people become more reluctant to
change as they gain more of a stake in the system
and have more to lose. There are other societies,
for example the Swedish, with age compositions
older than that of our own population, that have
shown considerable propensity for social innova-

tion and, conversely, there are many younger populations, such as in Latin America, in which rates of social change have been comparatively slow. Once again, the significance of age structure appears to be mediated by so many other historical, cultural, and economic forces that it is difficult to develop any clear paths of social causation.

Minorities

What are the consequences of declining population growth for our racial and ethnic minorities? Are these groups participating in the national decline of fertility? Let us discuss these in terms of religious (Catholic, Jewish) and racial (black) minorities.

Catholic fertility in the United States has been historically higher than the national average but has followed the national trend and in recent years seems to be converging. By 1966–70 Catholic fertility was only 13 percent above that of white fertility in general, and that difference has probably narrowed further since then. The doctrinal opposition to contraception has diminished greatly among American Catholics. Indeed, today the contraceptive practices of Catholics are virtually indistinguishable from those of non-Catholics. Even their attitudes toward abortion, although still less permissive than those of non-Catholics, are changing. It seems highly likely that the fertility of Catholics will converge with that of the general population perhaps within less than a decade.

Jewish fertility, associated as it has been with higher education, higher income, and urban residence, has been the lowest of the major religious communities in the United States. Estimates are not easy to come by, but it seems clear that Jewish fertility is well below replacement. Jewish women born in 1926–35 had lower than replacement fertility, and, judging from trends among other groups, their fertility is probably even lower today. Combined with losses through intermarriage and the aging of the immigrant generations, such low fertility has reduced the size of the Jewish population from its high of 3.7 percent of the U.S. population in the late 'thirties to below 3 percent today, and it is still falling. Whether this decline in numerical importance will reduce their status in American life or perhaps threaten their very survival is a current concern of prime importance within the leadership of the Jewish community.

The fertility of whites and blacks also shows some indications toward convergence. Although blacks as of 1975 were completing their families with about 3.5 births per woman compared with 2.9 for whites, young (18–24) black married women in 1975 expected a lifetime total of 2.5 births compared with 2.1 for whites. Actual fertility of young black women under 25 dropped by about half between 1960 and 1975. The fertility of women of Spanish origin was about halfway between that of white and black women and shows a similar downward trend. The link between proverty and high birthrates is considerable, and, as various disadvantaged minorities move into the mainstream of American life, their fertility as well as other behavioral characteristics will blend more closely with that of the majority. In addition to general economic and educational progress, government and private family planning programs seem to be making an impact judging from the fact that as of 1973 an even higher proportion of black than white married women practicing contraception were using the most effective methods. As of a 1970 study, nearly all of the excess of black over white fertility was due to the higher unwanted fertility among blacks in the past. These facts suggest an increasing convergence of race differences in marital fertility in the near future.

These demographic trends are not regarded with equanimity by all leaders of the black community. A vocal militant minority is very suspicious if not hostile toward government and private family planning programs, which at worst are viewed as genocidal in intent. Such an attitude is fueled by infrequent but well-publicized semi-compulsory sterilizations of young black women on welfare and by the appearance of birth control clinics without pediatric or maternal health clinics in black ghettos. Some blacks feel that the government is trying to use birth control as a cheap substitute for economic aid; still others feel that the most direct path to black political power is through increasing the numbers of black voters, as recent mayoral elections seem to have demonstrated. In the black population at large, however, the average woman is just as anxious to control her childbearing as her white counterpart.

In general, therefore, the rates of population growth of the main minorities in the country seem to be becoming more homogeneous, and we can anticipate a time, certainly before the end of the century and probably sooner, when group differences in population growth will be mainly of historical interest. The old idea of the "melting pot," now in disrepute because of reappearing ethnic identities, seems still to be a valid concept for understanding the homogenization of reproductive behavior.

Marriage and Family

In describing the decline of fertility, I alluded earlier to perhaps radically new changes in marriage patterns that may be developing. These changes are both cause and consequence of declining fertility. We are all somewhat vaguely aware of new mating patterns that seem to be emerging, which are becoming increasingly socially acceptable, of young unmarried people living together. We assume that such arrangements are intended to be experimental preludes to marriage. Between 1960 and 1976 the proportion of women not married by ages 20–24 has increased from 28 to 43 percent. In Sweden the number of marriages declined by nearly half between 1967 and 1973. In Denmark the number of young (20–29) unmarried couples cohabiting jumped from 200,000 to 300,000 between 1974 and 1976. No doubt the same development is occurring in many other Western countries. The intriguing question, of course, is whether we are witnessing a postponement of marriage with an institutionalization of trial marriages or a more basic change that will eventually alter the institution itself.

It is abundantly clear from our very high and still increasing divorce rate that the traditional concept of one partner forever has disappeared for growing segments of our society. The divorce rate, which increased by 45 percent between 1970 and 1975, has now reached the level where one of every three marriages will sooner or later be dissolved. That trend has hardly been regarded as a serious threat to marriage *per se* since such a large fraction remarry. This is still true, but there are signs of change. The remarriage rate, which has steadily increased over recent decades, has started to decline. (In Sweden it has declined by about 50 percent since 1965.) A higher proportion of second marriages now seem headed for divorce. Cohabitation is not limited to the young premarital state; one is increasingly aware of middle-aged and even older divorced couples living together without the formality of marriage. There are more and more "nonfamily" households (consisting of either individuals living alone or sharing quarters with one or more unrelated persons). Such nonfamily households accounted for nearly one half of the entire increase in the number of households between 1970 and 1976.

All of these trends which seem to be depressing reproduction, separating sex from reproduction, and weakening the permanence of marriage are tied in one way or another to the growing economic independence of women as well as to the diminishing influence of religion in our lives. There has been a substantial increase in the proportion of

women in the labor force, a trend that still shows
no sign of abating. Women still occupy a disproportionate share of the lower-paying jobs, but there
is little doubt that the future direction and significance is clear. In a matter of another generation or
two, a substantial fraction of women will have the
option of financial independence, although they
may still be earning less than men. It is difficult to
overestimate the significance of this trend for the
family. The institution of marriage will lose yet
another part of its sociological foundation. For centuries man has exchanged some of the financial
rewards, social status, and security associated with
his employment and income for the sexual, com-
panionate, and maternal services of women. This is
hardly a romantic view of the relationship, but it
does go a long way toward explaining the univer-
sality and historical persistence of marriage. But
consider a social system in which just as many
women as men are engineers, bank presidents, corporation executives, doctors, lawyers, salesmen,
and so on. What exactly will be the motivation of
women to enter the legal partnership of marriage?
Considering the ease of divorce and the growing
acceptability of simply living together, does it not
seem probable that traditional forms of marriage
will diminish even further than they have already?
One of the remaining sociological rationales for
marriage is having and raising children, but with
the retreat from parenthood that seems to be in process even this age-old rationale seems shaky. If
current first-order birthrates were to continue, about
30 percent of women would never have any children, an unprecedented but not totally implausible

development. There is now evidence that childlessness even within marriage is increasing. The proportions of ever married women aged 25–29 who had not yet given birth increased from 12 percent in 1965 to 22 percent by 1976. Moreover, if the large increase in illegitimate births that has occurred in Sweden in recent years as a consequence of unmarried couples living together is any indication of a diminishing taboo on having children out of wedlock, then even this function of marriage may be weakening. It seems significant that in the United States in 1975 there was a record high proportion (14.2 percent of all births) of illegitimate births, in which the greatest increases occurred among white women 20–29 years old. At the same time, the birthrate reached a new low.

Thus, demographic trends, more particularly the decline of fertility, can be regarded as both a cause and a consequence of changes in the family. The decline of childbearing can be construed as freeing women for economic equality with men, which in turn makes marriage and childbearing less of an automatic social response. The future seems less and less compatible with long-term traditional marriage.

Future Growth

If this prognosis is even roughly accurate, it raises the very basic question of how society is going to sustain the level of reproduction necessary to replace one generation with the next. Such questions are not new; they were raised 40 years ago during the depths of the Depression, when birthrates had fallen sharply and an impending decline in population was projected. At that time there was speculation by at least one serious sociologist that society would develop professional breeders, that reproduction would become the specialized function of a category of women who would be paid for their childbearing services. The products of such specialists would be raised in special child care institutions in the absence of conventional family arrangements.

This all has a ring of science fiction about it, and, of course, the war and the subsequent scramble to the suburbs, marriage, and the baby boom made the whole speculation seem ludicrous in retrospect. I am not suggesting that such a phenomenon will appear in our time, but if current trends continue, and, as I noted earlier, I see little on the horizon to suggest otherwise, there is little doubt that some types of financial incentives to encourage childbearing will have to be implemented as they already have, in mild form, in many European countries. And my guess is that there will have to be considerable public investment in underwriting such incentive systems. There is no clear evidence that the trivial baby bonuses, maternity care, and various employment benefits that have been legislated in European countries have had any appreciable impact on the birthrate. It is difficult to imagine well-paid women with little interest in childbearing being attracted by a few hundred dollars' worth of miscellaneous benefits. There may very well have to be a serious investment in child care institutions and in society's willingness to subsidize reproduction.

There is an alternative to subsidizing reproduction in order to meet the consequences of negative natural increase, and that is immigration. Assuming that our economy can remain strong enough
to attract immigrants, the desired rate of population
increase could be achieved through the manipula-
tion of immigration quotas, a practice not unknown
in our past. Since the supply of immigrants to the
United States typically exceeded existing quotas,
the qualifications of immigrants could be set fairly
high to bring in persons with training in short
supply in our economy. This concept already exists
in our immigration law. From the economic point
of view, such a practice would be highly reward-
ing, since the capital costs of education and training would have been borne by other countries.
From the social point of view, however, to depend
entirely on importing our population deficit would
have many of the problems that we associated with
the assimilation of immigrants in our past: different
customs and languages, additional minority group
problems, hostilities of many native citizens (50
percent of the public in 1971 thought that immigration should be reduced), and so on. It is instructive
that other countries confronted with such questions
have opted primarily for programs to raise the fertility of their native populations. The recent labor
migrations in Europe, and the difficulties of accom-
modating large numbers of foreign workers in
countries with labor shortages, has also been an experience that the receiving countries are not likely
to forget if it comes to the more basic question of
supplementing population growth.

Thus, immigration does not seem like a basic
long-term solution if the rate of natural increase

falls and remains radically below replacement. If current fertility rates were to continue beyond the time when zero population growth were reached, our net immigration volume would have to be about doubled in order to avoid population decline.

This whole discussion is predicated on the assumption that governments will not look kindly on negative population growth or, for that matter, even a sustained period of below-replacement fertility prior to zero population growth. It is quite obvious that negative population growth cannot be sustained indefinitely, although some of our citizens appear not to be averse to returning to a population about half our current size, which was the level experienced around 1920. We know very little about the short-run consequences of negative population growth; the long-run consequences are clear.

Conclusions

So what does it all add up to? Americans are having fewer children than ever before, and there do not seem to be any forces in view that would reverse this trend. Better contraception is available and is being used, and abortion is increasingly available. The demographic result is a rapidly declining rate of population growth and an expectation that zero population growth may be reached in 40 years and possibly sooner. Estimates for a total as low as 250 million persons are now in vogue. The age composition will change significantly with an increase in population of working age and of persons 65 years of age and older, and a decrease in youth.

In general, the social, economic, environmental, and political consequences of these demographic changes seem desirable. There are some concerns about the implications of an older population, but sooner or later as population growth slows such change is inevitable. Aside from those questions, the reduction of growth means less pressure on the environment and resources and an opportunity to invest economic growth in improving the quality of life. From the standpoint of economy, there will be more workers and fewer dependents, and per capita income will be higher. From the standpoint of government, there will be an opportunity to invest public resources in higher quality education and to improve the level of government services generally.

The future of marriage and the family is less clear. The divorce rate continues to rise, the marriage rate is down, and there seems to be a massive postponement of marriage in the making. Increasingly, young men and women are living together without the added commitment of marriage; illegitimacy rates will probably continue to increase. Whether increasing proportions will never marry or will just marry at a later age is unknown yet. Although it seems ironic, if not ludicrous, in view of our concerns about growth of only a few years ago, to be worrying possibly in the near future about *maintaining* replacement fertility, there are reasons to believe that some subsidization of reproduction may become necessary. Such a situation has been reached already in more than one European country, and the social trends apparent today all seem to point in that direction.

We should probably be more cautious in our

extrapolation of current trends. I reminded our inquiring journalist that it was less than a decade ago when strong antinatalist views were being expressed (licensing parenthood, rationing babies, infertility drugs, etc.), and certainly the current speculation will look silly if another baby boom occurs, but, it seems to me, the writing is on the historical wall. However, perhaps the most appropriate concluding observation is that of a colleague of mine who said: "Each generation seems to assume that the demographic circumstances it is experiencing will persist and tries to formulate population policies to ensure that they won't."

DISCUSSANT

Ernest Kurnow
Professor of Business Statistics,
New York University

In reviewing the essays by our authors I could not help thinking back to one of the early lab exercises in a statistics course with Professor Willford I. King more than 30 years ago. We were to fit five mathematical equations to census population data through 1930. In doing so we found that all five curves fitted the data almost perfectly. In addition, when the curves were projected to 1940 they all gave good estimates. However, when estimates for the year 2000 were made, the differences in the estimates ran into the hundreds of millions, because implicit in each curve was a different set of assumptions. We were to select the best estimate and were rated correct or incorrect by the professor in keeping with the prevailing opinion at that day, and, of course, I had the correct answer. Needless to say, our population today has already outstripped by far the "correct" estimate at that time.

Furthermore, if the same exercise had been repeated 15 years later we would have had a second correct answer, which would also be incorrect today. Now, another 15 years later, we find that the analysis by both our authors is based on the "correct" answer in the statistics class of today.

There are serious doubts, however, that the "correct" answer for 1977 will be correct 15 years from now. Why do I feel that way? In the first place, let us look at the historical record. Richard Easterlin, who has studied the record in great detail, finds that, although the trend in birthrates has been downward for a period of well over 100 years, as pointed out by Westoff, changes in birthrates have fluctuated upward and downward with swings from peak to peak ranging from 10 to 15 years earlier in the century and on the order of 35 to 40 years more recently. He concluded that these fluctuations could be explained as long cycle phenomena, characteristic, as pointed out by Simon Kuznets, of many types of economic data, and that substantial swings in fertility rates may occur again over the longer run. In other words, we might expect another peak at some time in the 'nineties.

In addition to the historical record, economists and sociologists are expressing doubts concerning the accuracy of the prevailing estimates. I'd like to present two illustrations, one from economics and one from sociology. As background for the economics illustrations, I'll return to my statistics class of over 30 years ago. We were told that birthrate was dependent on the relationship between an individual's scale of living and standard of living. Scale of living was defined as those goods and services which an individual's current income could command, and standard of living consisted of those goods and services an individual preferred to marriage and a family. Therefore, birthrates would tend to increase if the scale of living of individuals exceeded their standard of living, and decrease if the scale of living was less than the standard of living.

More recently, we find a variation on this theme proposed by Easterlin, known as the relative income hypothesis, which states that an increase in the current standard of living (scale of living in the King formulation) relative to the expected or desired standard of living (standard of living à la King) will result in an increase in fertility, while a decrease in the ratio will result in a decrease in fertility. The Easterlin version, however, has an advantage over King's in that it lends itself more readily to measurement.

Taking advantage of this fact, Michael Wachter developed a time series model to study fertility rates for the period 1925–72, incorporating the Easterlin ratio and other relevant variables. In 1975 he reported that his model reproduced the actual swings in fertility rates over the period and that it confirmed Easterlin's relative income hypothesis. He concluded that he is less sanguine concerning the inevitability of a further decline or even maintenance of current fertility rates that might be inferred from earlier writings. In fact, Wachter feels that current low fertility rates may merely be a reflection of a trough of a long cycle whose previous peak was the end of the postwar baby boom in the late 'fifties.

Sociologists are similarly expressing less sanguine views with respect to the inevitability of declining fertility. Judith Blake in a recent article points out that low birth expectations are incongruous with other American reproductive attitudes, namely, the tolerance for large families and the aversion to childlessness and the one-child family. She attributes the current decline in large part to the "unique stimulus of intense public attention to population and family size since the 'sixties." Illustrative of what she is referring to are books with such ominous titles as Ehrlich's *The Population Bomb,* with sales of more than 2 million, Price's *The 99th Hour Population Crisis in the United States,* and Paddock and Paddock, *Famine, 1975,* as well as the wide publicity accorded the "day of doom" forecasts of the Club of Rome. Blake did not provide empirical evidence for her assertions, but more recently David Kruegal did find evidence of the influence of this public bombardment upon attitudes toward family size.

A "counter-literature" appears to be developing backed by empirical studies to question the forecast of a continuing decline or leveling off in fertility rates.

I might also interject at this time that the "fast approach of a perfect contraceptive society," mentioned by Westoff, need not imply that fertility rates will continue to decline. If we were to pursue that line of reasoning we could end up attributing the baby boom of the 'fifties to the widespread prevalence of unwanted births—which I doubt that anyone would claim. Families were known to have had many wanted children during those years.

I would now like to direct my attention to a second aspect of the forecasts upon which our authors based their opinions. These forecasts generally deal in aggregates and not the composition of these aggregates. Very often the correct policy is not a function of the aggregate as much as of its composition.

To offer an illustration, both authors mention the expected decrease in the dependency ratio, which they view as highly desirable, because there will be relatively more people supporting relatively fewer people. However, the beneficial results of a low dependency rate cannot be inferred on the basis of aggregate figures alone. It is necessary to know the composition of the dependency class. To what extent will dependents be welfare recipients, and how will poverty be defined at that time to determine who qualifies for welfare? Empirical research indicates that, if we adopt a relative concept of poverty, the share of national income going to welfare will increase in the year 2000, even at a favorable rate of economic growth and under the population projections used by both our speakers. In that event, we would find ourselves worse off even with a decreasing dependency rate.

I turn now to another area of concern. Implicit in both essays is the assumption that a reduction in the rate of population growth is highly desirable. In fact, Professor Westoff regrets that the work of his Commission did not result in the adoption of a national population policy. The present state of economic knowledge, however, warrants no such conclusion. A review of the literature for the Commission on Population Growth led Allen

Kelly, who prior to that review favored an antinatal government policy, to conclude:

a. Attention to the lowering of fertility rates as a means of resolving major economic and environmental problems is unwarranted.

b. Persuasive quantitative research revealing a detrimental net impact of population growth on the pace of per capita income or consumption is lacking.

c. If social and/or individual welfare is taken as a norm of population policy as against material wealth, it is difficult to defend any policy other than a neutral one regarding family size, i.e., provide people with the requisite knowledge concerning birth control and let them decide for themselves on a proper course of action.

The literature since that time has done little to improve the state of our knowledge. In fact as recently as June 1976 Paul A. Samuelson and Alan Deardorff were still debating the optimum growth rate for population in articles in the *International Economic Review*.

Given the uncertainties that pervade this entire area, I feel that what we need is a set of scenarios based on different sets of assumptions. However, we should then resist the temptation to pick the correct curve or the correct answer but should formulate policies for each of the resulting states of the world. I believe that we would find that the policies fall into two broad groups: (a) those that would be applicable no matter what state of the world was predicted, and (b) those that would be applicable to a specific state or a few states.

The first group of policies should be proposed for immediate action, and the second group should be held in abeyance, given the current state of knowledge, for consideration on an *ad hoc* basis depending upon how the future unfolds—an approach, by the way, that Professor Cohen pointed out should have been followed with respect to social security legislation.

I would like to thank Professors Cohen and Westoff for their interesting and challenging essays. I further hasten to assure them that, when the year 2000 rolls around, I will rush to the videophone to extend to them my congratulations on the unusual accuracy of their predictions.

DISCUSSANT

Dennis H. Wrong
Professor of Sociology
New York University

Dean Cohen and Professor Westoff have traced for us some of the probable long-range economic and social consequences of the slowing up and eventual end of American population growth. Dean Cohen discusses not only the effects of changes in population growth and composition over the next 50 or 60 years but their implications for social policy as well, giving special attention to the financing of the social security system of which he himself was one of the authors and to the higher costs of medical care imposed by an older population. Professor Westoff concentrates more closely on the demographic trends themselves, especially future fertility, and suggests some of their likely consequences apart from possible policies designed to cope with and influence them.

I have little to add, nor any major objections, to their discussion of particular consequences. It is worth pointing out, however, that neither author deals with future trends in population distribution and their effects, as distinct from overall population growth. Professor Westoff does note at one point that "even with approaching stabilization, problems of the distribution of population will remain." In his closing remarks, Dean Cohen suggests that higher energy prices will intensify migration from the Northern industrial states to the sun belt, thus speeding up the shifts in regional political power that we have already begun to witness. Many of the problems that a few years ago were attributed to the so-called population explosion were actually due to a "suburban" or "metropolitan explosion": the clogging of transportation arteries, the overstraining of recreational facilities, the disappearance and defilement of the countryside adjoining old urban areas, increasing residential segregation of social classes and ethnic and racial groups, the fiscal crisis of central cities, and the decay of inner-city neighborhoods. Changes in population growth and composition are not likely significantly to alter the need to confront what my colleague Roger Starr calls "the shrinking city," at least in the Northeast and Midwest, nor the problems of expanding urban sprawl dependent on the automobile in such cities as Phoenix, Houston, or Denver. Policy dilemmas arising out of population redistribution may turn out to be far more politically troublesome than the problems posed by an older population with a low birthrate in view of the built-in potential for conflict in a territorially based system of electoral representation.

    Both Dean Cohen and Professor Westoff believe that present low levels of fertility will continue and bring about zero growth by the third or fourth decade of the twenty-first century. Both speakers can be described as optimistic about the effects of reduced population growth. Dean Cohen doubts that it will in itself curtail economic growth and hopes that it will encourage improved health, educational, and welfare policies. Professor Westoff also thinks that lower population growth need not depress economic growth and that it may even increase per capita GNP. In addition, he anticipates its having beneficial effects on environmental problems. Although I shall again at a later point briefly remark on the generally optimistic outlook of both authors, I wish to direct my remaining remarks primarily to the assumption they share that present low fertility will not be reversed.

Professor Westoff is, of course, properly skeptical about the ability of demographers, as indicated by their past track record, to forecast the future trend of fertility, although he clearly doubts the likelihood of any sharp reversal of the recent decline. He mentions, in fact, at the very beginning of his paper that it is the baby boom of the 'fifties which requires explanation rather than the resumption of a fertility decline that had begun in the nineteenth century in the United States as well as in other advanced industrial countries and was interrupted for only a little over a decade in the period after World War II.

I shall take him up on the question he raises about the baby boom, since he passes over it to concentrate on the implications for the future of declining population growth. In looking at the recent past instead of the future, however, my aim is not to offer anything that pretends to amount to an explanation of the baby boom but merely to suggest the complexity of the determinants of reproductive behavior today, their intimate interdependence with much else of a nondemographic nature that is going on in society and history. Far from being an autonomous realm, a partially independent variable, fertility trends now raise all the problems of social and historical causation that have long been recognized in the cases of other trends and changes in mass behavior such as attitudes toward work and leisure, shifts in popular culture, and so-called swings of the pendulum from Left to Right and vice-versa in political opinion.

If the baby boom of the 'fifties was demographically aberrant, it was consistent in this respect with a great many other things that happened in that decade. The 'sixties, especially the late 'sixties, witnessed the collapse of a number of assumptions that had seemed securely established only a few years before: belief in the fundamental benignity of American foreign policy and the agencies carrying it out, in the achievement of a domestic consensus summed up by the phrase "end of ideology," in the continuation of high rates of economic growth as a solution of all problems at home and abroad, in the virtual inevitability of rapid progress toward racial integration, and in the suburbanization of practically everyone into a middle-class, familistic, mobility-oriented way of life. The explosiveness of the challenge to these assumptions in the late 'sixties produced, of course, a "backlash'' that reached its zenith with President Nixon's overwhelming re-election victory in 1972.

Commentators have shown a tendency to regard the dominant trends and assumptions of the 'fifties as embodying the distinctiveness of American destiny itself. Their overthrow and reversal is therefore seen as a crucial watershed in American history. Such a view seems to me to be an over-reaction to recent events comparable to that of those journalists who are always asking Professor Westoff to explain the current decline of fertility as if *it* were the aberration or novelty and the preceding baby boom somehow the norm. But the 'fifties, after all, followed a world war and a catastrophic economic depression. They now appear to have been a brief interlude, a period of false calm between two times of troubles, standing in contrast to what preceded and succeeded them just as the baby boom represented an exception of short duration to a longer secular decline in fertility.

The militant protest movements of the 'sixties and the intense reaction against them have by now both disappeared, but there has been no restoration of the reigning beliefs of the 'fifties, just as there have as yet been no signs of a return to the higher fertility of that period. Moreover, many of the reforms of the 'sixties, such as changes in the laws governing civil rights, censorship, private discrimination against minorities, sex, abortion, marriage, and the family, appear to be for the most part irreversible, just as much of the New Deal became irreversible with President Eisenhower's election in 1952. Some of these reforms, as Professor Westoff notes, have created new structural supports for non-familistic life-styles conducive to the maintenance of lower fertility.

The congruence between the baby boom and so much else that was part of the 'fifties underlines the fact that preferences and values governing fertility behavior are inextricably interwoven with larger historical tendencies that are unique and irreducible. Perhaps the "law" proposed by economist-demographers of an inverse relation between cohort size and fertility will hold up, but I share Professor Westoff's doubts about it. I think it will meet the fate of that earlier, cruder, economistic "law" that fertility is directly related to the movements of the business cycle in proving to lack predictive value beyond the historical context in which it was originally observed to hold. Whatever may have been the case a half-century or more ago, the demographer cannot be expected to forecast future fertility trends with any confidence when they depend on so many incalculable "variables" that combine and converge in incalculable ways to give to a period the historical distinctiveness that we perceive only after it is over. Today one can only laugh at the hubris of the demographer who proclaimed in 1930 that "the population of the United States, ten, twenty, even fifty years hence, can be predicted with a greater degree of accuracy than any other economic or social fact, provided the immigration laws are not changed."

What the demographer *can* do with considerably more confidence is what Dean Cohen and Professor Westoff have done: indicate what some of the major consequences will be *if* demographic trends continue to move in more or less the same direction as at the present time. But in nervously reminding himself that he may be, like his more secure predecessors of a few decades ago, simply "eternalizing the present"—or, rather, the trend of the present—the contemporary demographer is not merely displaying a chastened sense of modesty but is, in effect, conceding that fertility behavior is now shaped by economic trends (including the price of oil and, for that matter, of eggs), cultural fashions and counter-cultural revolts, the political struggles of ideological and interest groups, the condition of international relations, the progress of contraceptive technology, and much else.

To foresee the course of all of these things, the demographer would have to be a prophet, and, if he were, we would probably want to ask him about more urgent matters than the future trend of fertility. He need not apologize therefore for confessing that he is unable to anticipate changes that might abruptly reverse present trends, even though he knows that, in Karl Popper's words, "a trend is not a law" and that long-established trends have often enough reversed themselves in the past. With respect to the future of fertility and American population growth, I find myself in exactly the same position as Professor Westoff in being unable to imagine what might plausibly happen to reverse the present trend—even if demographers, as his closing citation of a colleague's remark suggests, should decide that it ought to be reversed.

In addition to tracing the consequences of projected trends, the demographer can also indicate with some confidence the limits within which *pos-*

sible changes in fertility behavior are likely to take place. As Professor Westoff shows, the changes from the low levels of the Depression years through the baby boom to the more recent decline took place within a range of from an average of 3.5 births per woman at the peak of the baby boom to 1.8 at the present time. The difference hardly reveals any dramatic transition from small to large families and back again, although, as Professor Westoff notes and as the Report of the Population Commission of which he was executive director fully demonstrates, the aggregate effects of a three-child average family size as against a two-child figure will cumulate to produce very considerable differences in population growth over the next 25 to 50 years.

More than thirty years ago demographers failed to foresee the baby boom, because the low fertility of the 'thirties continued an eighty-year-old trend of declining fertility. They assumed reasonably enough that the new lows in fertility of the decade were the result of social tendencies long at work in industrial society rather than of the short-run impact of the Depression. Hence their readiness to conclude—prematurely but not necessarily inaccurately, as it *now* looks—that capitalist industrial society was inherently inimical to the family and procreation and that far-reaching pronatalist policies would be needed to avoid population decline. Their failure even to consider the possibility of a baby boom stemmed from their inability to disentangle the impact of short-run, transitory events from relatively constant but cumulatively effective influences in a situation in which *both* had the same—in this case, a negative—effect on fertility. This is an excellent example of what has been called, adapting a term of Freud's, the *overdetermination* of historical events and processes.

Critics of Professor Westoff's recent writings on fertility and of the Report of the Population Commission which he directed have suggested that fertility may have been depressed in the late 'sixties by transitory events comparable to the economic hardship of the 'thirties and that to look ahead to zero growth and its consequences is simply to repeat the earlier error. The tremendous media publicity given to environmental deterioration and its alleged connection with population growth and the sudden, often flamboyant, emergence of a new feminist movement may have encouraged delayed marriage and childbearing and smaller family size aspirations. I myself wrote a few years ago that the saturation of the American population by the mass media was such a new historical fact that public and official concern over the relation of population growth to the general welfare might now be exercising an unprecedented influence on the reproductive decisions of millions of couples.

But the alarmism over ecological doom and the "population bomb" has greatly abated, as has the volume of publicity received by the women's liberation movement, and fertility decline in any case both preceded and outlasted them. It is worth recalling that the low fertility levels of the Depression were themselves viewed with considerable alarm as contributing to a stagnant economy, whereas concern over the environment and resource shortages has meant that the present decline is generally regarded as a boon rather than a threat. The fact that two such influential experts as Dean Cohen and Professor Westoff view the prospect of declining population growth with equanimity and even with optimism is notable. Neither of them is surveying the scene from an ivory tower, both having already made significant contributions to social and economic policy and to governmental consideration of policy goals. Their counterparts back in the 'thirties took a far different and gloomier view of the prospect of a long-term declining population growth, which seemed as imminent then as it does today. This is in itself an important difference from the earlier situation and one that works in favor of the continuation of the present trend. It may be, as Professor Westoff suggests, that demographers and social scientists will shortly start worrying about the implications of a protracted "birth dearth" and succeed in generating a new alarmism that is pronatalist in its emphasis. But at the moment the contrast between the present and the anxiety over incipient population decline in the 'thirties remains striking. Moreover, we live in a larger world today: If it is not quite McLuhan's "global village," we are nevertheless less prone to consider our own population trends in isolation from those of others, including the peoples in the underdeveloped countries, who constitute a considerable majority of the world's population.

APPENDIX

The charts and graphs in this section are from the U.S. Bureau of the Census, *Current Population Reports,* Series P-25, No. 601, "Projections of the Population of the United States: 1975 to 2050" (Washington, D.C.: U.S. Government Printing Office, 1975).

Table A. ESTIMATES AND PROJECTIONS OF TOTAL POPULATION: SELECTED YEARS, 1940 TO 2025

(In thousands. As of July 1. Includes Armed Forces overseas)

Year	Series I	Series II	Series III
ESTIMATES			
1940........		132,594	
1945........		140,468	
1950........		152,271	
1955........		165,931	
1960........		180,671	
1965........		194,303	
1970........		204,875	
1971........		207,045	
1972........		208,842	
1973........		210,396	
1974........		211,909	
PROJECTIONS			
1975[1]......	213,641	213,450	213,323
1976........	215,653	215,074	214,613
1977........	217,891	216,814	215,895
1978........	220,327	218,678	217,285
1979........	222,938	220,663	218,783
1980........	225,705	222,769	220,356
1985........	241,274	234,068	228,355
1990........	257,663	245,075	235,581
1995........	272,685	254,495	241,198
2000........	287,007	262,494	245,098
2005........	303,144	270,377	247,926
2010........	322,049	278,754	250,193
2015........	342,340	286,960	251,693
2020........	362,348	294,046	251,884
2025........	382,011	299,713	250,421

[1] Due to the entry of Vietnamese refugees and to a sharp drop in mortality rates in the older ages, the estimated population for July 1, 1975 -- 213,631,000 -- is above the Series II projection.

Figure 1. Estimates and Projections of the Population of the United States: 1940 to 2025

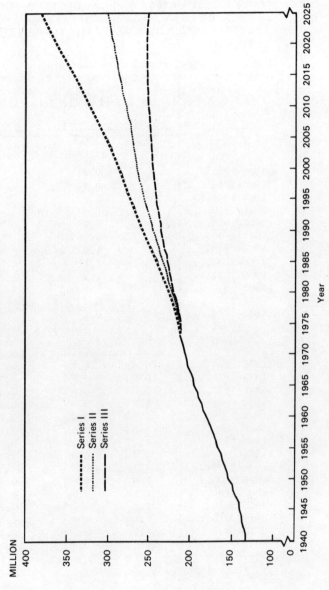

Table B. ESTIMATES AND PROJECTIONS OF AVERAGE ANNUAL PERCENT CHANGE IN TOTAL POPULATION: SELECTED YEARS, 1930 TO 2025

(Includes Armed Forces overseas)

Years (July 1-June 30)	Series I	Series II	Series III
ESTIMATES			
1930-1935[1]....		0.7	
1935-1940[1]....		0.7	
1940-1945....		1.2	
1945-1950....		1.6	
1950-1955....		1.7	
1955-1960....		1.7	
1960-1965....		1.5	
1965-1970....		1.1	
1970-1971....		1.1	
1971-1972....		0.9	
1972-1973....		0.7	
1973-1974....		0.7	
PROJECTIONS			
1974-1975....	0.8	0.7	0.7
1975-1976....	0.9	0.8	0.6
1976-1977....	1.0	0.8	0.6
1977-1978....	1.1	0.9	0.6
1978-1979....	1.2	0.9	0.7
1979-1980....	1.2	0.9	0.7
1980-1985....	1.3	1.0	0.7
1985-1990....	1.3	0.9	0.6
1990-1995....	1.1	0.8	0.5
1995-2000....	1.0	0.6	0.3
2000-2005....	1.1	0.6	0.2
2005-2010....	1.2	0.6	0.2
2010-2015....	1.2	0.6	0.1
2015-2020....	1.1	0.5	0.0
2020-2025....	1.1	0.4	-0.1

[1]Excludes Alaska and Hawaii.

Source: Table A, and Current Population Reports, Series P-25, No. 521, tables 5-6.

Figure 2. Estimates and Projections of Annual Population Change: 1940 to 2025

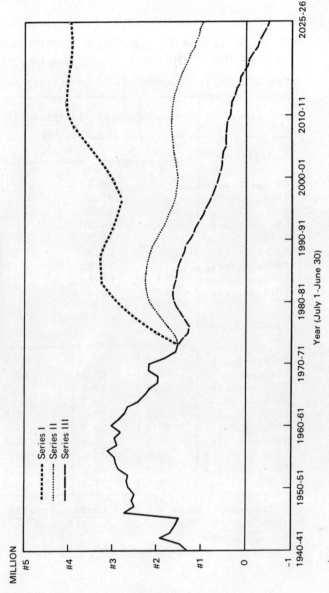

TABLE C. ESTIMATES AND PROJECTIONS OF THE MEDIAN AGE OF THE POPULATION: 1950 TO 2000

(As of July 1. Includes Armed Forces overseas)

Year	Series I	Series II	Series III
ESTIMATES			
1950.........		30.2	
1955.........		30.2	
1960.........		29.4	
1965.........		28.1	
1970.........		27.9	
1971.........		27.9	
1972.........		28.1	
1973.........		28.4	
1974.........		28.6	
PROJECTIONS			
1975.........	28.8	28.8	28.8
1976.........	28.9	28.9	29.0
1977.........	29.1	29.3	29.4
1978.........	29.3	29.5	29.7
1979.........	29.4	29.7	30.0
1980.........	29.5	29.9	30.3
1985.........	30.1	31.1	31.8
1990.........	30.8	32.3	33.4
1995.........	31.4	33.6	35.2
2000.........	31.4	34.8	37.0

Source: Tables 6-9, and Current Population Reports, Series P-25, No. 311, and No. 519, table 1.

Table D. ESTIMATED AND PROJECTED SEX RATIOS BY AGE: 1974 AND 2000

(Males per 100 females. As of July 1. Includes Armed Forces overseas)

Year and series	All ages	Under 5 years	5 to 13 years	14 to 17 years	18 to 24 years	25 to 34 years	35 to 44 years	45 to 54 years	55 to 64 years	65 years and over
ESTIMATE										
1974.........	95.4	104.4	104.0	103.8	101.4	98.5	95.7	93.4	89.5	69.8
PROJECTIONS										
2000										
Series I.....	95.3	105.3	105.2	105.0	102.4	98.7	96.1	95.4	90.7	64.9
Series II....	94.5	105.2	105.1	105.0	102.3	98.7	96.1	95.4	90.7	64.9
Series III...	93.8	105.2	105.1	104.9	102.1	98.7	96.1	95.4	90.7	64.9

Figure 3. Estimates and Projections of the Population of the United States, by Age and Sex: 1974 and 2000

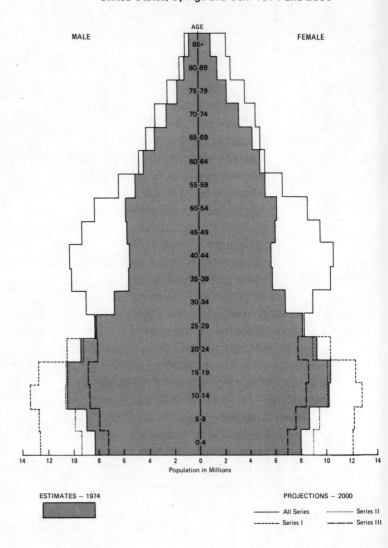